CHASING 22

FIRST EDITION

Designed by Meridith Feldman, Skylographic Design

ISBN: 978-1-7324607-0-6

ACKNOWLEDGEMENTS

This book would not be possible without the help of my family, friends, students, clients, mentors and colleagues. Special thanks to my friends David Green, James Parmiter and Lois Moran for their constant feedback, as well as Rob Lentini, Andrey Axelrod, Mavis Jaye, Jim Buchanan and my brilliant son Jordan Phillips. This was a challenging book to write, not simply because of the content, but because of the unusual demands in my life over the past 7 years. Therefore, a very special thank you to my best friend Nicole and my beautiful daughter Julia, both of whom served as endless sources of encouragement for me. Finally, thank you to my editor Ellen Peixoto and my graphic designer Meridith Feldman of Skylographic Design. I have worked closely with Meridith for nearly 10 years on various projects including 13 different editions of my Ultimate Transformation Challenge manuals (available for public purchase fall of 2018). The visual layout of Chasing 22 took a lot of time and organization. As you read, I hope you find all the effort involved in getting this book into your hands well worth it!

CONTENTS

PREFACE

The information in this book is dense, but easily digestible. It has been compiled in such a way to make you think deeply about topics that are remarkably important, yet often ignored. I've done my best to give ample insight into many complex matters, but by no means is any section a true end-all testament of the subject. This is why the book is so heavily footnoted. It is my way of encouraging each reader to delve deeper. Resources cited include documentaries, TV series and movies as well as various podcasts and YouTube videos. I did my best to use the most interesting and credible experts in their appropriate field to make my points, but I chose the bulk of these information sources for a unique reason. First, I want facts to be easily accessible and also fun to watch or hear. Second, I want young adults of this generation to receive this information and feel empowered to investigate these topics. Dredging through a lot of peer reviewed dissertations to find data is usually the opposite of fun for the casual reader and certainly to most young adults. Instead, I chose books, articles and peer reviewed research more carefully and only when necessary. You will see the book is divided into an introduction and then 4 parts. If parts are skimmed or ignored or read out of order, it is an absolute certainty the reader will miss the extreme relevance of the points that come later. I am banking on the fact that if you pay attention, you'll learn something remarkable about yourself and the world around you. My hope is that you'll share what you learn with your friends, family, students and teachers. After all, the goal of this book is to serve as a catalyst to greater conversation on a vast array of very worthy topics. Now, stretch your mind and get ready to *Chase 22*.

CHASING-22
A Thinker's Search for Free Will

by Thomas Phillips

We want information, information, information.

Who are you?

The new number 2.

Who is number 1?

You are number 6.

I am not a number, I AM A FREE MAN!!!!
[Laughter]

Patrick McGoohan's 1967 television series The Prisoner
(Episode 2, "The Chimes of Big Ben")

INTRODUCTION

Human beings are endowed with a sense of curiosity. In our continuous search for information, the type of information sought is often not pragmatically useful; instead we merely look for escapes or avoid important conversations altogether. In the dialogue above, the question, "Who are you?" couldn't be more existentially profound. But the answer is a number, followed by ominous laughter at the claim of being "a free man." This likely sounded mysterious to viewers of *The Prisoner*, undoubtedly because they didn't put much thought into its implications; however, the case for freedom is difficult. If you never thought about the various aspects of freedom, you're not alone. But I contend one particular aspect of freedom is the single most important principle to explore in order to understand one's self and the world in which we live. In the spirit of metaphor, I chose twenty-two categories by which to examine this single aspect of freedom, what we call "free will." Questioning this sense of agency may begin to feel like a catch-22. It becomes disturbing for most, but by the end of this book you'll find the process quite empowering. But *catching* 22 first requires *chasing* 22. In this case, we will be chasing twenty-two "prisoners" of free will.

Think of anything you've ever tried to accomplish in your life and failed. Maybe you got on the right track but couldn't keep going? As the owner of a fitness and wellness facility for nearly twenty years, I've authored many exercise and nutrition manuals that helped hundreds of people lose significant amounts of weight, get strong, and feel healthy. I've watched some of the same people put more than half of the weight back on and watched others avoid exactly what they need to do altogether. Nineteen years teaching math and philosophy to emotionally disturbed adolescents ensured that my master's plus-30 in education as well as degrees in History, Math, and English did not go to waste. Although I was making a small fraction of what I made as a business owner, I was and still remain passionate teaching those most difficult to reach. This hobbyhorse helped round out my 80+ hour work week. But teaching these troubled students also allowed me another unique insight into human behavior. I watched many young adults come out of darkness, become great students, live normal productive lives, only to commit suicide or overdose within ten years of graduation. I'm fascinated—and distressed—by this, but I also understand the reasons. More importantly I know most *do not* know why they fail or continually sabotage themselves.

The "IS-NOTness" of Life

While authoring this book I lost a dear friend to suicide. My friend, Eric Arauz, was fairly well known in public speaking circles. His funeral included a eulogy from former governor Jim McGreevey, as well as many other doctors and politicians whom Eric helped influence positively. Eric's book, *An American's Resurrection*, saved many lives. Despite his knowledge, one crisp, clear, and slightly cool Saturday night in late March 2018, Eric could not save his own life from the pernicious darkness that intermittently permeated his mind. Through no free will of his own, Eric was the victim of an abusive childhood and a crippling mental illness known as bi-polar disorder. On that night, during those highly vulnerable hours, the ephemeral darkness Eric knew his entire life, took his life. As a result, his wife lost a husband and his daughter lost a father. What took Eric's life? Who killed the thirteen students I knew to suicide? Merely thoughts. That's it—thought alone killed those kids and most recently my friend. Eric used to talk about the "Is-ness" of life, but over time I recognized that Eric's version of "Is-ness" did not include the most important component of human existence—namely, the "Is-ness" of what **IS NOT**.

The Punch You Don't See
Is the One That Knocks You Out

By having a very clear understanding of what free will IS NOT, we gain a huge advantage over our minds. This requires a dramatic shift in thinking, but lack of knowledge is the proverbial blind-sided punch that puts most of the population on its back. Upon understanding every facet of the *actual* problems regarding free will, you will become disturbed, but you will also see the punches coming and thus be better prepared. Along the journey, you will learn a tremendous amount of practical information about yourself and the world around you.

I certainly recognize that statements arguing against free will sound counterintuitive, but was quantum physics intuitive? Do the interactions of electrons consume your conscious awareness at any given moment of the day?

Yet it is the undeniable underlying reality in which we participate. To discover that realm we needed the right questions and the right technology. Today, we have impeccable tools to probe the human mind, body, and world around us; however, very few are asking the right questions. Even fewer are willing to implement pivotal knowledge gained from objective science. How can an individual or a society make progress if our ambitions are relegated to fantasy and our minds subject to complacency? Again, if we can't even see the punch coming, how do we prepare for its imminent impact on our lives?

> He can leave at any time. If his was more than just a vague ambition, if he was absolutely determined to discover the truth, there is no way we can prevent him. I think what distresses you, really, caller, is that ultimately Truman prefers his cell as you call it.
>
> —Christof, *The Truman Show* (1998)

The similarities between Patrick McGoohan's 1967 television series *The Prisoner* and the 1998 movie *The Truman Show* are remarkable. But in The Truman Show, the character Christof (played by Ed Harris) was "Christ of" the town Sea Haven, a clear play on words for "see heaven." Truman (played by Jim Carrey) was the unknowing prisoner born into a bubble-like world. In order to break free, he had to become a "true man." After thirty years of monotony, Truman's questions and careful attention to detail allowed him to face his fears. Soon he was face-to-face with the inconvenient facts surrounding his existence. Like Odysseus, he survived the proverbial storm at sea. After his battering from "the man in the sky," his persistence was well rewarded. His hero's journey complete, he quite literally exited the stage to a standing ovation.

> The seeker should not stop until he finds. When he does find, he will be disturbed. After having been disturbed, he will be astonished. Then he will reign over everything.
>
> —Jesus, *The Gospel of Thomas* (saying #2)

I promise you will leave this book as a more enlightened individual; however, like Truman, how we get there will be an unusual journey. You will not know where we are going. You will not know how we will get there, but please allow me to lead, because I will not stop until you find. But first you must become disturbed, then you will be astonished. Finally, in the end, I promise a destination—a "promised land." To succeed we will need an open mind, endurance of spirit, and a willingness to embrace inconvenient facts. As you read, you will gradually cultivate more compassion for your own self and others. From here, we can draw an accurate map of the mind's landscape— then we can enter the territory prepared for meaningful conversation, but more importantly, meaningful action.

Are *you* ready to break free?

The seeker should not stop until he finds.

The Role of Doubt

When I was eight years old I remember wondering how Santa got to every kid in only one night while finding time to enjoy milk and cookies. I recall feeling disturbed when kids received much more than me. Was this because Santa could see what I was doing? If so, can he read my mind? I wondered why I never saw his flying sled or the reindeer with the shiny red nose. I would ask myself, "If I don't have a chimney, will Santa come through the front door?" Then I remember it hitting me all at once: "It's all make-believe." As soon as that thought crossed my mind I knew it was true. I didn't need further validation. I quickly concluded the Easter Bunny, the tooth fairy, and the rest of the imaginary characters in my childhood were an illusion. But a unique illusion—an illusion in which parents and society collaborate. This grand illusion was created for the sake of a tradition that claims, "It's more fun for kids to believe."

Getting Comfortable
with Doubt and Disturbance

This was the first time I appreciated an important emotion in my being, the emotion of doubt. Modern neuroimaging shows the feeling of doubt creating stimulation in the anterior insula part of the brain, an area synonymous with disgust.[1] It's also the area of the brain that lights up when people believe they might be about to make a mistake.[2] The emotion of doubt and the feeling of making an imminent mistake both seem to be on a spectrum of repugnance within our awareness. Growing up, both scenarios moved high on my emotional "disgust

> "
> I think it's time we get comfortable with disturbance, errors, and doubt.
> "

spectrum." The older I got, the more invested I became in certain beliefs; therefore, the more disturbance I felt as I meticulously unpacked errors within those beliefs. I think it's time we get comfortable with disturbance, errors, and doubt. More importantly, I think it's possible to embrace these feeling in a beneficial way. After all, if we can get better at something, we should get better at objective reasonable human conversation.

The Washing Tongue Adventists

Who cut down the cherry tree and never told a lie? I heard that story in first grade. I grew up believing George Washington was the most truthful man in American history, but simply because I never thought about it after first grade. Studying history in college, I heard my professor say, "George Washington was a successful general because he was an amazing liar."[3] This statement did not create a sense of disgust in me, instead it cultivated intrigue. But why? What was the difference in this circumstance? There are several:

- First, I was not invested in Washington being the most truthful person in American history; I could not have cared less.
- Second, the credibility of the person (history professor with a PhD) superseded a childhood story from my first-grade teacher.
- Finally (and perhaps most relevant): Something in me knew this alternate story made sense. No longer a first grader, but a well-informed young man, I quickly reasoned Washington was human. As a general he certainly would have used tactics such as deception to succeed.

Washington used an elaborate spy network and would regularly break traditional ethics of warfare, often employing appalling tactics unheard of at the time (such as sniper attacks on enemy officers). I remember hearing all the specific stories and feeling exuberance instead of doubt. I felt empowerment instead of anger. I felt inspired to learn more instead of feeling like I needed to plug my ears with my fingertips. However, let's take one more step in this dialogue.

Imagine an American religious cult still fully invested in our forefather's vision of the "city on the hill." They are vehemently opposed to lying and choose George Washington as their idol. They call themselves the "Washing Tongue Adventists," because they believe Jesus will not bring his kingdom to America unless we stop lying. They have elaborate lodges where they meet and tell stories about Washington (likely as truthful as the cherry tree tale). They have elaborate rituals, one of which includes putting exact replicas of Washington's wooden teeth into the mouths of their followers (symbolizing that words crossing our teeth must be truth-based), then making the faithful suck on a single sweet cherry with the wooden teeth, then violently spit out the cherry. This is done to remind them that, although tempting, never eat of the forbidden fruit called dishonesty. Imagine this organization continues to hold up Washington as the model life by which to live in order for Jesus to make his return.

My question is twofold. First, does living a truthful life necessitate the worship of Washington? In other words, aren't the benefits of living a truthful life self-evident once all facets of lying are weighed? Second, aren't these zealots missing the entire point of what Washington actually did in real life? Aren't they missing the *truth* of his brilliance and creativity in the midst of what seemed an impossible war to win? Imagine knowing what you *now* know about Washington, but each time you walk into a food store, the Washing Tongue Adventists are trying to get you to "suck of the cherry and spit." How would this strike you? More importantly, how would it strike them if you laughed and announced, "Your account of Washington's life is completely misguided." Can you imagine the state of *their* anterior insula at that moment? And this is precisely the point. As soon as we recognize these brain phenomena are not serving anyone interested in a constructive conversation, the easier it is to make headway. Therefore, going forward, let's approach the topic of free will with the mindset that there is something much greater to be discovered without misguided "brain stuff" getting in the way. After all, if we wish to be right about something, we must keep open the possibilities of being wrong. If we do, I think you will be satisfied with the "proof in the pudding"—but you need not put your wooden teeth in to taste what I'm offering.

Understanding Mistakes

Washington was a real person. The Washing Tongue Adventists and my first-grade teacher had interesting interpretations of this man. It would be a mistake to say there was no George Washington, but it would also be a mistake to say there is no Santa. After all, every December 25th there were presents under my tree. But the source of these magical powers resided much closer to home (literally). It is more accurate to say: The concept of Santa Claus exists, but for children, Santa is not who youngsters are conceiving in their immature, inexperienced, and vulnerable minds. In time, children come to understand this illusion through proper questioning, honest discourse, direct experience, and contemplation.

> Similar to an eight-year-old's impression of Santa Claus, or a Washing Tongue Adventist's notion of George Washington, free will is not what most people believe.

Similar to an eight-year-old's impression of Santa Claus, or a Washing Tongue Adventist's notion of George Washington, free will is not what most people believe. In fact, society has not bothered to question, discuss, or even have a direct experience with what they can unambiguously claim to be free will. And certainly, even fewer have taken all the evidence for contemplation.

1. Free will is an adult Santa Claus: He exists in a way that you don't conceive and is closer to home than you can possibly imagine.
2. Most people's understanding of Free will exists on a spectrum of bad beliefs no different than that of a Washing Tongue Adventist's.

PART II

When he does find, he will be disturbed …

Chasing Prisoner #1.
To Be or NOT to Be –That IS the Question

Have you ever paused to consider the abundance of human suffering on this planet today and throughout history? From a Buddhist (and largely Eastern point of view), existence is the problem, with enlightenment offering the only way out of this wheel of birth and rebirth. In other words, according to most Eastern traditions, being born is undesirable and not being born again is the ultimate goal. As far as free will, we can begin by acknowledging you didn't choose to be born, and you certainly didn't choose to be born into a bad situation. Human suffering is what compels individuals like Professor David Benatar to write his book, *Better Never to Have Been: The Harm of Coming into Existence.* Such deliberation about existence was at the forefront of philosophical minds throughout history and remains in debate today. In fact, the movie *Infinity War* (from the multibillion-dollar Marvel Comic series), has a plot loosely revolving around this issue. The villain Thanos believes half the creatures in the universe must die in order for life to thrive. For anyone willing to listen, his reasons are compelling, but this belief begs a much deeper question evidenced in Benatar's book; namely, would those individuals have been better off not being born in the first place? But not only for the benefit of everyone alive, for their own benefits as well, as dictated in many Eastern religions! Meanwhile, you may be wondering: Why? If

> As far as free will, we can begin by acknowledging you didn't choose to be born, and you certainly didn't choose to be born into a bad situation.

you fall into that category, please pay attention, because while some of us were busy contemplating philosophy, writing interpretive essays on George Washington, or hanging Christmas stockings, this next section will continue to disturb you (as advertised).

Born into Bad Situations (most of the time)

Orphanages in Romania have been overcrowded for decades and remain so today. From the late 1960s onward, the unfortunate children in orphanages were not held, not played with, barely went outside, and were often found in the fetal position, rocking themselves back and forth in overcrowded rooms filled with other youngsters suffering the same fate. If you watch *The Story of Us*, episode 3, "The Power of Love," you can see these heinous conditions for yourself. This atrocity is also mentioned in David Eagleman's book, *The Brain: The Story of You*.[4] These same orphans often develop IQs in only the 60s or 70s. Over two thirds of any population will have an IQ between 85 and 115. An IQ of 70 or lower puts a child in the bottom 2%.[5] These orphans also experience severe language delays and, often, lifelong social abnormalities. Of course, none of these children were born into a Romanian orphanage of their own free will. If you object to my narrowing the human experience to such an exaggerated tale of tragedy, then consider the following. More than 83% of the world lives on less than $20 a day. More than 70% of the world lives on less than $10 a day.[6] Over 90% of the world's HIV-positive children live in Africa.[7] Approximately 3.5 million children die each year between the ages of one month and four years.[8] Again, no sane person would choose to see their child die, nor would anyone choose to be born into these circumstances according to their own free will–and yet we are talking about over five billion people on this planet who fit into some or all of these categories! If you don't fit into these categories, thank your lucky stars– but please don't have the hubris to call it good karma or God's will; instead, let's simply acknowledge that things need to change. Nevertheless, the analogy of Romanian orphanages is meant to be an example of human suffering for circumstances described below, but by no means is it an outright exaggeration of human suffering on the planet today or throughout history.

Dr. Charles Nelson's research examined children removed from

Romanian orphanages before the age of two. These children had a much better chance of a reasonable recovery, which is a testament to the power of the brain and, more specifically, to the miracle of neuro-plasticity. Consider that by the age of two, humans have nearly twice as many neurons in their brain than they do as adults. This process of neuronal pruning begins naturally and without conscious effort. The brain did this continuously to get rid of what we seemingly "didn't need" or "weren't using;" this is the brain's way of doing what it does best: maximizing efficiency. After all, the brain is wired to survive, not perform. Therefore, the axiom "use it or lose it" has strong implications here. Rescuing orphans before the age of two is crucial, because from that moment on, the critical period of neuronal pruning is well under way.[9]

Chasing Prisoner #2.
"Groupness" and Bigotry

But age two is important for another reason. Judith Rich Harris's research has shown that by the age of two (and certainly by three), children have a strong desire "to do what other children do in a group." And what constitutes "groupness" is alarmingly simple if you read chapter 7 of her book, *The Nurture Assumption*.[10] What children do in groups is extremely similar all over the world and throughout time. In fact, her work focuses on how little parenting has to do with child development compared to the environment in which a child finds himself or herself (the concept of "groupness" being just part of this environment). Thus, if a child begins to do what other children do by the age of two, being rescued before this critical juncture to reasonably assimilate back into the world makes sense. Again, if a child is left in the orphanage after the age of two, it is only a matter of time before they rock themselves back and forth and mimic the dysfunctional behaviors of other children surrounding them.

Groupness plays a darker, more disturbing role in the human mind. Harvard psychiatrist Mina Cikara studies how people move from individuals, to groups to bitter rivals.[11] Like Judith Rich Harris, Mina has discovered how easily adults will exhibit "in-group bias" with something as arbitrary as assigning random red and blue team colors. If this seems overstated, take a trip to a Red Sox vs. Yankees or Giants vs. Eagles game and look at what's going on in the stadium. A more revealing situation played out catastrophically in an Iowa third-grade classroom on April 5th, 1968. The day after Martin Luther King Jr. was assassinated, Jane Elliot decided to teach her students about the problems with bigotry. First, she separated blue- and brown-eyed children. Next, she gave her class a seemingly reasonable "scientific" explanation as to why brown-eyed kids are smarter than blue-eyed kids. Finally, she made the blue-eyed kids wear green construction paper arm bands; she also made them drink from paper cups for fear the brown-eyed kids would "catch something." Soon, kids were crying, behaviors were changing rapidly, and a rift within the classroom was imminent. After the weekend, she reversed the experiment; again, with another clever explanation. Now on the other end of the bigotry, more crying and more dramatic behavioral changes among the children. The exercise soon made national news. What transpired fifty years ago is still talked about today and put Ms. Elliot on the historical map of behaviorism.[12]

Schadenfreude: Pleasure Derived from Another's Misfortune

The brain is wired to survive, not perform. As a result, bigotry (especially in situations where you are asked to make fast decisions) has been hardwired into us at levels we are only beginning to understand. Underneath, Mina Cikara suggests a combination of media and television bias, as well as our necessity to group together to survive and/or feel an identity, influences our decisions.[13] These characteristics have been true throughout human history. Yet this primal instinct has created an unreasonable animal brain, more specifically seen within our ventral striatum. The ventral striatum is the seat of addiction in the brain; in fact, we can learn to crave experiencing our rival's discontent, as evidenced in sporting events—or bad divorces, for that matter. The Germans even have a word for it: *Schadenfreude*. Next time you're at a sporting event or participating on a team yourself, step back and watch the show as "reasonable" adults with young children turn into maniacs. In fact, if you ever see *me* compete, you'll see a deluxe version of *schadenfreude*!

Modern neuroscience has established that the fully developed human brain (including the frontal cortex) doesn't come completely on-line until about age twenty-five.[14] Now, knowing how incredibly vulnerable the brain is by the age of two and all the way up to twenty-five (and even after twenty-five if you decide to become a sports fan or participate in team competition), simply take a moment to ask yourself:

- Did you pick your parents? Your genes? Your gender? Your socioeconomic status? Did you choose to be born in the United States? Did you choose your siblings? The toys you played with before the age of three? Did you choose to be born into a family where mom and dad loved each other? Did you choose your neighbors or the elementary school you attended? Did you choose the kids that would be in those classes? Did you choose your teachers? The questions go on.

But let's go even farther back:
- While pregnant, what your mother ate (or didn't eat) had remarkable effects on your brain development and physical structure. A quick study of fetal development during the Dutch winter famine between 1944 and 1945 will make this point abundantly clear. Among other things, the famine affected infant size at birth as well as central nervous system development. Obviously, these pregnant mothers had no control over their lack of nutrition, yet their children still suffered.
- More compelling research shows that a pregnant mother's emotional well-being has astounding effects on an unborn child's emotional predispositions. According to Dr. Thomas Verny (world-renowned expert on this topic), "Everything the pregnant mother feels and thinks is communicated through neurohormones to her unborn child, just as surely as are alcohol and nicotine." Did you have anything to do with your mother's drug or alcohol use? Did you have anything to do with her diet or levels of stress or anxiety at her time of pregnancy?

By acknowledging how significant environment is to a fetus and up to the age of two, while conceding how little any of us could do about our own personal environments at that time, we can begin to appreciate some of the problems surrounding free will.[16]

> 66 Acknowledging how significant environment is to a fetus and up to the age of two, while conceding how little we could do about our personal environments at that age, we can begin to appreciate some of the problems surrounding free will. 99

But it does not end here. Not even close.

Chasing Prisoner #3.
Head Trauma and the APOE4 Gene

The NFL and other combat sports are in the midst of addressing the unfortunate and largely unforeseen realities of head trauma. Some will argue these athletes engaged in dangerous activities "according to their own free will." But what about the children who fall off their bikes and slam their heads on the pavement?[17] What about my own father who suffered a heat stroke then fell face first into a concrete driveway? Within a year his acts of aggression were evident. The damage to his frontal cortex was painfully obvious as he ceased being Bill Phillips and started to become someone we did not know.

Furthermore, those in possession of a common APOE4 gene polymorphism are much more likely to suffer an unfavorable outcome from a traumatic brain injury (TBI),[17] including its probable synergy in the development of Alzheimer's disease.[18] The APOE4 gene is a "double whammy," because having this polymorphism and getting hit in the head with a ball could prove catastrophic! Accidents happen without free will; similarly, we are born with certain undesirable gene polymorphisms without free will, yet both circumstances are on a spectrum of debilitation that could profoundly alter how we function in the world. More importantly, if we can do something about it, we should! I go into detail about genes, epigenetics, and some polymorphisms (as well as how to test for them) later, but here is a quick take away: If you or your loved ones have this APOE4 polymorphism, then staying away from actives that can induce head trauma is highly advised!

When TBI Is a Blessing

When Jason Padgett was mugged and struck in the head, his once-mediocre math brain awoke to discover an incredible new ability.[19] Everywhere Jason looks, he sees the world in a particular geometry; more specifically, everything he sees is made of triangles. This insight allows him to solve complex problems at a genius level as well as draw intricate pictures using triangles that are truly dumbfounding. Google his artwork and see for yourself. Similarly, Derek Amato suffered a traumatic brain injury after diving for a football in the shallow end of a pool. Having been severely concussed and hospitalized, Derek would take weeks to recover. About a month later, Derek did something extraordinary. While in his friend's house, Derek walked over to a small electric piano and just started playing as if he had been playing the piano his whole life. He did this for almost six hours. At one point Derek looked up to see his friend's astonished face, his eyes filled with tears.

What Do Jason's and Derek's Injuries Say about the Brain?

For Jason, head trauma equated to mathematical and artistic insight while Derek's head injury sparked musical ability. Later you will hear about Daniel Tammet, whose seizures as a young boy led to a condition that allowed him to speak a foreign language within only one week of exposure (and with no accent!). Why is that? Because math, music,

> These stories should make us pause to process the way the brain is organized. Take a moment to appreciate the possibilities that exist within this three-pound tool sitting between our ears.

and words are all forms of language. They all require a great deal of practice to develop these skills (at least in normal circumstances), yet head injury can make this process inexplicably efficient. These stories should make us pause to process the way the brain is organized. Take a moment to appreciate the possibilities that exist within this three-pound tool sitting between our ears.

Feeling Lucky? I Bet It All on Black 22

No sane person would randomly hit themselves with a ball-peen hammer and hope to awake with Jason's mathematical prowess; they'd be much more likely to suffer the same fate as my father (or worse). But why do similar events affect people so differently? How can anyone avoid head injury when we have a head that can be struck by anything at any time? The best we can do is be more cautious. But let's call this what it is: *luck*. As you continue to read, and from what you already read, take a moment to consider the role of luck in every scenario and how this continuous random "rolling of the dice" maps onto free will.[20]

> ... consider the role of luck in every scenario and how this continuous random "rolling of the dice" maps onto free will.

Be aware that luck is *easily* misunderstood. There is a big difference between luck as "anomalies" (as described above) and mistakenly assigning special significance to "coincidence." I write about anomalies in more detail later, but I promise coincidence is not a special spiritual message from the heavens. To illustrate the point, here is a recent true story. In a seminar, I spoke about coincidence in a joking context. Afterward, my client Bruce told me about the *Baader-Meinhof phenomenon*. I looked it up and sure enough, the Baader-Meinhof phenomenon is when you suddenly hear or notice something and soon it seems to crop up everywhere. A week later, I was meeting with my client Lois at Whole Foods. She was telling me a story and asked if I ever heard of *schadenfreude*. I had never heard the term. Her husband is German, so she told me its meaning. I said, "Hmm, have you ever heard of the Baader-

Meinhof phenomenon?" She said, "No." I explained what it was and said, "Watch, within a week I'll hear about Schadenfreude, and if I do I'm finding a way to put it into my book!" Sure enough, three days later while researching a particular study in the *Through the Wormhole series* (season 6, episode 1) at exactly 22:38, the word schadenfreude comes out of Morgan Freeman's mouth! I immediately texted Lois; the Baader-Meinhof phenomenon was in full effect and as a result, you are hearing about *schadenfreude* for a second time.

Statistically Not Special

Looking into Kate Kirshner's work, *What's the Baader-Meinhof Phenomenon?* will give insight as to how this occurs in the brain; however, a basic understanding of mathematical probability is also helpful. For example, in a bar, when do odds turn favorable that any two people in the room have the same birthday? Since there are 365 days in a year, you might assume 183 people. But the answer is only twenty-three. It may seem impossible, but it is mathematically correct. And when these types of seemingly random/special events occur, it is *not* a sign of fate. Instead, it's just understanding how the brain *actually* works biologically and how the world *actually* works mathematically. Often what seems to be a special coincidence is not that special after all.[21]

Chasing Prisoner #4.
The Verdict Is In: Hunger?

What could food have to do with free will? More than you can imagine, as you will discover later in this book! But here, I'm not talking about specific foods per se. I'm talking about the feeling of hunger. How much does hunger shape our behavior in the world? For starters, there is a reason why eating a good breakfast correlates to better test scores in standardized tests; who wouldn't opt for more brain power? But extremely relevant stories come out of the court house. If we hold up a voice of reason in the world, hopefully we would choose a judge, or someone of that caliber. Yet studies of 1,112 parole board hearings in Israeli prisons have shown that judges are far less likely to grant parole just before lunch and just before end of day.[22] This may seem remarkable, but it should feel concerning. If a judge, whose education and experience can lead to such dystopian acts of justice because of low blood sugar, then by all means, Judge, please have a sandwich! Who would want a "hangry" judge deciding their future? Furthermore, which prisoner would want to invoke their "free will" by raising their hand at 11:30 a.m. to ask, "Um, Judge, did you eat lunch yet?"

"I Meant to Say That, I Think?"

Of course, the more important implication is free will. If you were to ask the judges about any particular decision, the science explained below shows they would likely give fantastic answers;[23] however, their rationale simply doesn't match with the odds of the data. The truth is, their low blood sugar affected their decision making. As a result, would-be parolees were denied probation and put back into prison—again, all as a result of an insulin imbalance in the bloodstream of the judges upon whom their fates hinged. But confabulating the reason for behaviors post-hoc happens all the time and for many different reasons! For example, the smell of garbage makes people's answers to provoking questions measurably more conservative. More telling, if you ask why they chose a certain answer (say a month ago) compared to now, participants give compelling tales as to why they did it. No! That's *not* why they did it. It was the environment. It happens over and over in studies, and yet we as human beings continue to come up with ways to substantiate why we do what we do. But this is a microcosm of how the brain is working all the time. Robin Hanson's book, *The Elephant in the Brain*, is devoted to demonstrating how the brain confabulates excuses to do what it just did; the book has a treasure trove of studies.

> ... would-be parolees were denied probation and put back into prison—again, all as a result of an insulin imbalance in the bloodstream of the judges upon whom their fates hinged.

Finally, taking the time to understand different parts of the brain is extremely helpful. For example, cutting the corpus callosum[24] (a procedure to prevent grand mal seizures), or damage to the ventral medial prefrontal cortex both demonstrate how impressively these areas deal with rationalizing action. Yet, regardless of brain health in these areas, upon further investigation, the truth claim for motive is often purely fabricated. As you will read later in the book, taking time to learn how to watch your mind can reap big rewards; taking time to see how the mind is always in the mode of justifying its last behavior is quite incredible.

Chasing Prisoner #5.
Sick and Tired of Being Sick and Tired

The previous section explained how something as simple as blood sugar can affect agency, even in critical decision making; however, a lack of sleep will prove more detrimental. According to neurobiologist Matthew Walker, we need a minimum of seven hours of sleep each night, yet 50% of Americans fall short of this benchmark.[25] In a previous section, Alzheimer's disease was discussed with its correlation to the APOE4 gene. Recent studies reveal that an under-slept lifestyle equates to a significantly higher risk of Alzheimer's.[26] This may seem like staggering news, but once you study the importance of sleep, lack of sleep is yet another form of brain damage caused by the aggregation of beta-amyloid plaques around neurons and within neuronal synapses. According to Dan Pardi, MS, followers of an under-slept lifestyle are 55% more likely to become obese and suffer the burden of a chronically impaired immune system. Other undesirable outcomes include:

> " ... if you're among the 50% of Americans living an under-slept lifestyle due to insomnia, narcolepsy, a newborn baby or emotional distress, pause to recognize that the consequences of poor sleep are through no free will of your own. "

poor mental and physical performance, higher likelihood of addiction, increased occurrence of heart attack, and even the development of cancer![27] Therefore, if you are one of the 50% of Americans living an under-slept lifestyle due to insomnia, narcolepsy, a newborn baby or emotional distress, pause once again to recognize that the consequences of poor sleep are through no free will of your own. Worse still, overnight laborers or those working 24- to 30-hour shifts (such as firefighters or surgeons) often suffer deleterious effects to themselves and others! For example, an under-slept surgeon is 170% more likely to make a major mistake in the operating room. A residential surgeon working a 30-hour shift is 430% more likely to make a diagnostic error in the intensive care unit. In a strange twist of fate, that same residential surgeon is 168% more likely to get into an accident on the way home and return to the same hospital they just left, where yet another under-slept surgeon may be preparing to operate on them![28] If your loved one happens to be the victim of vehicular manslaughter due to that exhausted residential surgeon's micro-sleep cycle while behind the wheel, it would certainly be through no free will of the doctor; in fact, the 30-hour work cycle policy should be held culpable. But if your loved one was a victim; this bit of data post hoc would offer little condolence.

Now you may wonder, how did this infelicitous medical practice come about in the first place? Why does it continue in many areas? The answers to that conundrum are more sinister and are covered in a later Prisoner. But part of the answer may reside in the fact that on average, medical doctors only get about two hours of education on sleep,[29] despite the fact that their patients spend about one third of their lives in this critical state. If Prisoner #5 is concerning to you, then keep reading, because later in the book many answers to improve your mental and physical health through better sleep are on offer. Upon catching such a consequential prisoner, one may begin to feel like a more salient, conscious agent in the world.

Chasing Prisoner #6. Hardware Problems as Mental Illness

Earlier, I discussed how the anterior insula affects our ability to reason, but the acute onset of a mental illness can throw human reason out the door completely, along with the entire garbage bag. Hearing John Nash, one of America's most brilliant mathematicians of the past 100 years speak about his experiences with schizophrenia is quite mesmerizing.[30] In his early 30s, John suffered from abrupt delusional thoughts and behaviors, so much so that he was let go from his teaching position at MIT. Later he was hospitalized and subject to extreme forms of treatment, including insulin coma. About four years later, John got markedly better and began working again, but he would still write things like, "Rational thought imposes a limit on a person's relation to the cosmos." And he would call his remission periods, "interludes of enforced rationality." All of this while publishing papers at Princeton University. Furthermore, in the documentary *A Brilliant Madness*, you hear John say, "To some extent, sanity is a form of conformity."[31]

At first glance, these look like the statements of a madman. But even when John was healthy minded he was known for thinking in ways that nobody else thought; he always tackled the math problems nobody wanted to touch. Upon solution, his colleagues would realize that John's approach was 180 degrees the other way—nobody would have thought to do it the way John did it. But, of course, this type of thinking was not unique to John Nash; in fact, this is what makes great thinkers. Einstein's theory of relativity for example, disproved the Newtonian view of the universe ticking like a "big grandfather clock." The view of *one second, one second, one second* seemed totally obvious and made sense in everybody's experience. Yet today, we know that speed and gravity influence our experience of time. If there is one thing any scientist would agree on, it's that reality is not based in common sense. If it were, we would have a unified theory, we would understand consciousness, quantum physics, the origins of the universe, and so much more. So, a second look at these quotes from Nash warrant curiosity as to what was happening in that brain when he spoke the words, "To some extent, sanity is a form of conformity." After all, when I discuss synesthesia later, the experience a synesthete is having

> " ... a second look at these quotes from Nash warrant curiosity as to what was happening in that brain when he spoke the words, "To some extent, sanity is a form of conformity. "

when reciting pi out for 20,000 places is not from memory but instead from a landscape of mind that breaks all conformist approaches to mathematical computation. But for John, his most profound utterance came much later.

After a couple of decades grappling with the voices in his head, John Nash seemed to be completely cured. A remarkable phenomenon, but not unheard of with this disease. When John was asked, "How did you get better?" his answer, if true, has profound implications. John's words were simple, direct, and serious: "I willed it." John simply decided he would no longer be a victim of these voices in his head. Reading this, you may be thinking, *Ah, you see? He used his own free will to break the chains of this mental illness.* First, I caution that if you truly believe that, then map it onto the larger population of the mentally ill. Imagine President Trump getting on TV and saying, "No more disability for the mentally ill, stop being a bunch of mental midgets and get back to work; after all, if John Nash could do it, you all can." I recognize some of you reading this can envision President Trump doing precisely that, but the point is larger. Because as much as it appears to be John's free will, "willing" his way back to mental health, as you will see later, this is also happening due to no free will of his own.

Chasing Prisoner #7.
Hardware Problems as Mental Illness

But what about a tumor? As it turns out, a tumor on the amygdala will accurately predict acts of violence, sometimes extreme. Charles Whitman[32] is the classic example used in many books, so for the sake of simplicity I'll briefly rehash it here, but I'll also put a different spin on this story after you read the facts.

In the summer of 1966, Charles killed his mother and his wife the next day. He then shot sixteen people with a rifle from the 28th floor in a University of Texas observation tower. An autopsy revealed that Charles did, in fact, have a tumor on his amygdala. Was Charles acting according to his own free will? With what you know about the biology of the human brain, was he even culpable for these actions?

There is a twist in the argument that many free will advocates will be quick to point out. Charles suspected something was wrong with him; he was suffering terrible headaches for which he sought treatment, but never returned to the doctor. In what amounted to be a suicide note, Charles requested an autopsy of his brain. He then went on to kill his mother, his wife, and all of those people from the tower. It would be easy to suggest that Charles should be held culpable for his actions, because if he had insight into his problem, then he should have called for help or called the police or went back to the doctor. After all, if he can write a note, he can certainly make a phone call, right?

Jim Fallon has spent his career studying the anatomy of the brain with an emphasis on psychopathic killers.[33] His findings reveal a very definite and unique pattern in the brain: amygdala, anterior temporal lobe, orbital cortex, medial prefrontal cortex, cingulate and hippocampus. Looking at this anatomy in a diagram, you will notice a big connected loop. These areas are very much "turned off" in the brains of psychopathic killers. Jim Fallon explains, "Psychopaths walk around without feelings of empathy or emotion; instead they see people as forms that are no longer people." Furthermore, Jim estimates that at least 40 genes contribute to psy-

> " ... at least 40 genes contribute to psychopathic brain patterns. Almost all these anatomical patterns and gene expressions are indicated in the brains and biology of the violent killers Jim studied. "

chopathic brain patterns. Almost all these anatomical patterns and gene expressions are indicated in the brains and biology of the violent killers Jim studied. Since Charles Whitman had a tumor pushing on critical areas within this "loop" including the amygdala and orbital frontal cortex, it is expected that Charles would feel the effects of such brain damage, which includes:

* Extreme aggression
* Inability to plan his behavior
* Total insensitivity to punishment

Charles's writing a note instead of calling for help is not proof of his premeditation; instead, it is indicative of exactly this type of brain damage. Again, through no free will of his own, Charles seems to be a victim here–

as much as every unfortunate soul on campus that day.

But there is one more problem. As it turns out, Jim Fallon ran brain scans on himself and his family to check for predictors of Alzheimer's disease. To his utter astonishment, Jim has the predictive brain patterns of a violent killer, including the amygdala and orbital frontal cortex. To make matters worse, he also had the genes expressions to go along with a family history of murders. Yet, Jim Fallon is a highly accomplished neuroscientist living a happy, satisfying life with his family. Finally, a case for free will? Not quite.

As it turns out, this is where nature, nurture, and the feelings of groupness really matter. Jim Fallon grew up in a loving household; he had an extensive family that loved him, nurtured him, and gave him wonderful opportunities to grow. Charles, on the other hand, grew up with a violent and abusive father. In fact, Charles's mother left his father because of his mistreatment (mind you, at a time when it was unfashionable to separate or divorce). Charles also spent a considerable amount of time in the Marines as a sharp shooter. Childhood abuse maps onto the formula for violent criminals, and Judith Rich Harris would likely point out that Charles' "groupness" (with a rifle in hand almost every day as a soldier) eventually had something to do with his later actions. Later in the book I give genes and epigenetics their full due because this part of the story is missing here; but suffice to say, Charles was behind the 8-ball of free will the entire way down. I'm inclined to predict that anyone who could have had the misfortune of being this man, along with his history and hardware problems, would likely find themselves behaving in much the same way—due to no free will of their own.

Chasing Prisoner #8.
Hardware Problems All the Way Down
(Via Sam Harris)[34]

Regardless of your stance for justice in this scenario, it is critical to acknowledge that the problem was in the "hardware of the brain." Consider how many aspects of hardware problems can exist in the brain at any level. Schizophrenia, OCD, TBI, and PTSD are just a few examples of many types of hardware problems, yet these mental crutches can prove debilitating for the millions who suffer. As Sam Harris correctly argues, from this point of view, human suffering can begin to look like hardware problems at any given point along the flow of brain function.

For example, consider a baseball pitcher who can't get the ball across the plate. He complains of no physical problems other than his inability to perform the task. If we only look at where the pitch is going and judge him on where his pitch crosses the plate, then we are missing a lot of important information. What if the pitcher's thoracic spine and neck are extremely tight? Although he has no pain, tightness in these areas would equate to a pitcher missing the target more often than not. The problem is in the hardware of his body, and the pitcher doesn't even know. Similarly, any of us could have hardware problems in any region of our brain and never know. Charles Whitman didn't know; however, he did suspect something

> ... tightness would equate to a pitcher missing the target more often than not. The problem is in the hardware of his body, and the pitcher doesn't know. Similarly, we could have hardware problems in our brain and never know.

was wrong. If you suspect something is wrong with yourself, it may be a hardware problem. But even if you don't suspect something is wrong, there still may be a hardware problem. Consider the narcissism in society today—the ability to take responsibility for anything is becoming a lost art. For example, a single mother choosing to stay out until 2:00 a.m. five nights a week to binge drink while her teenage children are at home is, in fact, a problem. The mother either acknowledges this or not, but the power of the human mind can cultivate extreme forms of denial. However, this does not eliminate the probability of a serious hardware problem. In fact, the denial of a severe diagnosable medical condition is called anosognosia.[35] Many schizophrenics and people with bipolar disorder suffer from it; as a result, their ability to be self-reflective on their behavior is practically nonexistent. Ironically, this is also the main reason why they do not seek treatment. Therefore, whether you experience the hardware problem or not, Sam Harris's argument for hardware problems all the way down holds a lot of water.

Chasing Prisoner #9.
The Sea Captain and a Bunch of "Bull-Ship"

With that preamble out of the way, let's examine the best-case scenario for free will. We would be talking about a human brain at full maturity (about age twenty-five). We will assume it is free of tumors, traumatic brain injury, and, oh yes, a brain with normal blood sugar levels. At best, we can discuss "degrees of freedom" in which to operate.[36] Think of degrees of freedom like your joints. There are certain joints that are hinge joints, like elbows. They do not enjoy the same degrees of freedom as ball and socket joints, like wrists or ankles. The argument would be that, despite limitations, a person with constricting circumstances in life can still experience certain degrees of freedom as opposed to others with better options educationally, financially, socially, and so on, who can be exposed to far more experiences, ways of thinking, and overall degrees of freedom.

One may pause for a moment and ponder the universal justice governing the appalling circumstances some people are born into (through no free will of their own), but nevertheless, even the highest degrees of freedom are constricted like a cast around that ball and socket wrist joint. The environments in which we grew up as well as the interactions we had, the movies we watched, the books we read, the mistakes we made, the traumas we suffered, the teachers we loved or hated, the bullies we ran from, the kids who humiliated us, the baseball that hit us in the head, or the pet we loved but was struck by a car—all of this shaped our ability to perform a true willful act.

But let's give this concept its full due. For example, some authorities like philosopher Daniel Dannett insist that although a sea captain can't control the weather or the winds, he can control the ship. In other words, the sea captain has degrees of freedom in which to operate despite the circumstances. Dan put forward this argument in Sam Harris's Waking Up podcast (episode #39). This sounds like a reasonable notion. It sounds empowering, but let's start by acknowledging the circumstances about his ship and then revisit the metaphor.

- First, the captain of the ship did not grow the trees for the wood that made the ship. After all, quality wood makes a significant difference in the durability of a ship.

- Second, the captain did not have control over who designed the ship, cut the boards, or put the ship together. He did not know who created the sails, who inspected the sails, or who made and inspected the ropes tied to those sails.
- Third, although the captain may have had the privilege of selecting his crew, he certainly does not have control over their actions, especially in times of extreme desperation. Nor does he have control over their habits on any given day. If, for example, the weather looked clear on a particular night and the crew was in the habit of secretly getting drunk in the privacy of their cabins, this behavior would prove catastrophic if a storm blew in unexpectedly.

So, the captain finds himself in a vessel made of wood. Wood he did not grow or select. Wood that was put together from designs he did not create. The construction of the ship was commissioned by workers he did not know. Similarly, the ropes and sails were not made by him. His crew may have been selected by him, but his control of their actions is minimal.

Similarly, you find yourself in a vessel called a body. Most of the functions of the body are happening without your conscious awareness. When we get sick, for example, we are certainly not choosing illness; instead it's a condition of the vessel you find yourself in. But a vessel that you did not choose, design, or even ask to have!

The parallel of the captain in the ship is compelling to the human condition. Going back, let's restate what the captain does not have control over: the weather and the winds. Yet we now recognize that the captain has far less control over his circumstances and almost no control over his immediate environment as well. One may continue to argue he can still control his ship to some degree. Let's look at this more carefully.

If we say the captain can still act according to free will, his actions would be based on what? They *must* be based on everything he learned up until this moment as the storm crashes upon them. For example, it would matter whether the captain was born a Romanian orphan or the son of a great naval sea captain with a well-rounded education at his disposal. Let's bring the argument full circle. Did the captain choose his parents? His socioeconomic status? His teachers? Did he choose whether he was held as an infant? The questions continue.

Again, all the same questions will inevitably influence what the captain

> Is the captain consciously selecting his movement patterns and controlling his vestibular system as he frantically pulls the sails down while holding his balance in a rocking boat on a slippery deck with wind and water in his eyes?

will do. But even in doing, who is authoring his physical actions? The captain? Is the captain consciously selecting his movement patterns and controlling his eyes and vestibular system as he frantically pulls the sails down while holding his balance in a rocking boat on a slippery deck with wind at his back and water in his eyes? Of course not; we know there is an underlying mechanism driving these behaviors. Just as we know we are not consciously growing new skin cells, there are different underlying mechanisms driving movement as well.

Sean Carroll on the Bull Ship?

In a Sam Harris *Waking Up podcast* (episode #124), Sean Carroll (famous theoretical physicist) put forth a seemingly reasonable understanding of free will:

> Plato would have said there is something called a platonic form of a chair and this chair participates in that form. Today we know that's not true. The chair is made of atoms, but we don't say, "therefore there is not a chair," or "therefore the chair went away." There's a description of the chair as a chair (the level we describe it as chair) and another level below where we describe it as a collection of atoms. I see no incompatibility with saying there is a way of describing human beings (which is the best way we have, given the data and information we have about human beings in our everyday lives), which describes them as agents capable of making choices and also if we knew more about the micro processes within the brain we would use a different vocabulary for describing what they do.

But is this analogy between chairs and humans really true? I will reinstate my argument on "Bull Ship." Yes, we can talk about atoms as atoms and chairs as chairs. It's meaningful to do so and today, no educated person would argue the underlying reality of a chair is atoms. However, mapping this onto a human mind and free will is as incompatible as saying, "Specific parts of a ship are irrelevant to a sea captain's successful navigation." Unlike atoms in a chair, things actually go wrong in the building of a ship. A missing screw, a warped board, an area where the adhesive agents were compromised, and so on. These mishaps become a big deal in a storm; in fact, the entire boat can sink due to its weakest link. Sim-

> Unlike atoms in a chair, things go wrong building a ship. A missing screw, a warped board, an area where adhesive agents were compromised, and so on. These mishaps are a big deal in a storm; in fact, the boat can sink due to a weak link.

ilarly, a human mind suffering from any or all combinations of the twenty-two prisoners discussed in this book is victim to the output of its wiring in such a way that often one is left trying to make sense of one's own behavior. This is especially evident when witnessing a confabulated post-hoc justification for damaging actions after an emotional "storm." Just because we feel as if we are making choices does not mean we have free will; because just as we feel like we are thinking our thoughts, we certainly are not consciously choosing those either. The previous statement is investigated more rigorously in Prisoner 21 (*You're Not Who You Think You Are*), but Sean Carroll's argument is probably best nullified in the work of Robin Hanson's book, *The Elephant in the Brain* (referenced earlier in Prisoner #4).

Chasing Prisoner #10.
Acting Like the Actor on the Stage

Dr. Dennis Shaffer at Ohio State University studied the science of human movement for many years. Dr. Shaffer's research on movement while pursuing flying objects (such as catching a Frisbee) led him to conclude, "Our findings are showing we have no free will… And the reason is because their conscious awareness does not lock up with the mechanisms that guide their behavior while they're intercepting flying objects."[37] But we need not access Dr. Shaffer's work to have this insight for ourselves. All we need to do is step back and witness anything the body is doing at any given time. It is not hard to discover that it performs effortlessly as you peel an orange or open pistachio nuts. Each step along the way you think you are authoring a process, but look more closely. The orange seems to almost peel itself, the pistachio seems to come out of the shell with no precision of conscious effort on your part. This is how we operate almost all the time. A sort of autopilot that the nervous system has engaged in order for the mind to do what it does best: practice efficiency. But it is critical to note: The mind only gets good at what it practices. I will show you, later in this chapter and throughout this book, how alternative ways of going about mundane processes can open a floodgate of insight to willing practitioners.

> This is how we operate almost all the time. A sort of autopilot that the nervous system has engaged in order for the mind to do what it does best: practice efficiency. But it is critical to note: The mind only gets good at what it practices.

Chasing Prisoner #11.
Interpretations of Stress

Most important, storms and catastrophic circumstances offer the untrained mind and body the least amount of free will. Dr. Robert Sapolsky is one of the world's most highly regarded researchers on stress. In his book, *Why Zebras Don't Get Ulcers*, Sapolsky explains in phenomenal detail that how a stressor is interpreted matters![16,38] Interpretation is a learned response via many factors, but one of them is through social interaction. This is how a Navy Seal can learn to react one way to stress, while someone else will wet their pants and run for the

> This is how normal suburban young men turned soldiers can morph into a mob of rapists and pillagers in times of extreme stress, as seen in the Vietnam War.

hills. This is how normal suburban young men turned soldiers can morph into a mob of rapists and pillagers in times of extreme stress, as seen in the Vietnam War. A reading of the book *Achilles in Vietnam* by Jonathan Shay will give full testimony to these facts.[39] Nevertheless, consider how significantly even benign social interactions influence "who we want to be in the world"—and on any given day! For example, if you are on a diet and some jerk has the gall to bring cookies to work for someone's birthday, you don't eat one, but eight! Quickly you feel awful and likely angry at the bastard who brought those damn cookies in the first place! Again, you had all the right intentions of losing weight; similarly, young men sent overseas had *no* intention of becoming rapists and pillagers, yet the imposed environment dictated actions.

Chasing Prisoner #12. Technology

More immediate to your present environment, take a look at the smartphone within arm's reach of you. Computer programmer and Stanford University graduate Tristan Harris held a position at Google suspiciously titled "Design Ethicist." I remember listening to Tristan on a Sam Harris podcast,[40] then listening again to take notes. According to Tristan, the ability for programmers to drive attention on smartphones is remarkable, so remarkable that an ethics team was put in place. The morality of "how far down the rabbit hole" programmers drag attention while users mindlessly shop and sift through social media was the main agenda of his committee. I encourage you to read Tristan's article, "How Technology Is Hijacking Your Mind."[41]

Step back and consider these underlying facts. If computer programmers can manipulate attention so predictably that an ethics team had to be put in place, then consider all other manners of trickery in the world driving notions of free will down other rabbit holes.

> " If computer programmers can manipulate attention so predictably that an ethics team had to be put in place, then consider all other manners of trickery in the world driving notions of free will down other rabbit holes. "

Everything from the way a politician uses his hands, or how a televangelist uses his voice with just the right body and facial expressions to evoke a particular emotion in an audience giving him his ratings. In the words of Harry Plinkett, "You may not have noticed it, but your brain did."

Chasing Prisoner #13.
Your Senses and Your Mouth

Mouth

Indeed, the brain does an amazing job at superimposing meaning onto random objects and sounds through no free will of your own. For example, draw two objects below. One a smooth outline of a peanut and the other a star with 4 sharp edges. One is called a moomba and the other a tack-tick. Can you tell which is which?

If you are like most people, you assume moomba is the smooth-shaped object and tack-tick the jagged drawing. But these objects and words are make believe. When I first heard professor V. S. Ramachandran[42] speak on this topic, I was amused. But it turns out the explanation is more amusing. According to Dr. Ramachandran, the reason implicates our mouths and tongues. Observe your mouth when saying "moomba" out loud (go ahead, do it!). Now, observe your tongue saying "tack-tick." To keep it simple, one is smooth sounding, the other sharp. You did not need prerequisite knowledge to know which was moomba and which was tack-tick, your mind did it for you. What's more fascinating, you recognized which symbol was which without speaking the words aloud. You did this through no free will of your own. The mind simply recognized "smooth" and "sharp" and immediately mapped that onto the word choices

Hearing

Musical notes strung together evoke similar consequences. Hollywood is well-aware of this craft. Using a chord known as the minor major 7 (A, C, E, G#)[43] builds suspense during a high-tension moment in a thriller. A music theory class will expose such emotional manipulation in songs, TV, movies, and certainly commercials. Again, through no free will of your own, an emotional cascade is being superimposed, but this time via your ears. Every time you shop, watch TV, or listen to the radio, consider how music is hijacking your emotional state. This strategy leads to more liberal decisions to spend money or to "tune in next week." But if there's that smell of garbage nearby, maybe you'd be much less likely? What is for sure, you'd be able to give some highfalutin' answer for your choice!

Touch

Neuroscientist Henrik Ehrsson created an extraordinary experiment.[44] He had a person lie on their back in a bed with a set of goggles. The subject was to remain as still as possible. The video feed into the goggles fooled the person to believe he/she was looking at their own legs, but in fact it was a set of dummy legs in the bed next to them (exact same pants, shoes, etc.). A series of strokes coordinated between the two sets of legs and the appropriate sensations led each person with the goggles to believe there was nothing suspicious; they were convinced they were looking at their own legs—but they weren't! At first, they were just nice brush strokes, but as soon as the legs were threatened with a large knife, the individual's face cringed. But it didn't stop there. As the knife lightly touched the legs, they were convinced the sensation was happening to *them*—but nothing at all was touching their legs! In other words, the brain was superimposing a physical sensation based only on what it was seeing.

Smell and Sound

Smell often works in tandem with other senses in powerful ways. In the show *Brain Games*, season 4, episode 7, "Food," a food truck is set up with the words "Roadkill Café." When customers come over they are offered three items: opossum poppers, blackened beaver tail, and iguana lasagna. As you would expect, nobody is interested; however, when speakers were installed to amplify the sound of the sizzling and the cook fanned the flames to deliver smell into the crowd, people started purchasing the food! Stop for a moment to appreciate how appetite was influenced in this study—it seems from sound and smell alone— but these sensory inputs are triggering far more relevant culprits in your brain; in this case, the hormones ghrelin and leptin. Further information on this topic will be discussed in Prisoner #15 (*Epigenetics*), *Mouse Study* #2.

Taste

In another scene of that same *Brain Games* episode, three food experts were brought in and blindfolded. They were given five different foods to sample, and despite the inability to see their foods, each expert identified them correctly. However, once their sense of smell was taken away, the experts only got two out of fifteen correct. Clearly, taste occurs in concert with the help of other senses including smell. Pause for a moment and imagine how dramatically impaired taste is in individuals suffering severe allergies, or those prone to higher histamine levels.

Finally, remember the experiment with moomba and tack tic earlier? It turns out, sound is also implied in flavor. Given the words *lomba* and *kitiki*, which would go with creamy milk chocolate and which would go with a bitter dark chocolate? Likely you said kitiki for dark chocolate and *lomba* for milk chocolate. But why? According to Sri Sarma from Johns Hopkins University, this phenomenon is called sound symbolism. The brain automatically equates soft-sounding language like *lomba* with softer tastes like creamy milk chocolate. This scenario along with Dr, Sarma's full explanation can be viewed in *Brain Games*, season 4. episode 2, "Language." This topic is discussed later in more detail in Prisoner #15 *(Epigenetics)*, *Hitting the Tongue; Going, Going, Gone!*

Sight

Consciousness expert Anil K. Seth and Sam Harris discussed fallacies in sight during a podcast.[45] A well-documented experiment took pictures of a park (with people, trees, etc.) and had volunteers sit and stare at the scene. Little by little experimenters would gradually change the color of the sky, remove a tree, remove a person, a bench, and so on. Eventually the first picture looked

> " Metaphorically, this scenario shows a considerable perturbation of the human mind. From birth through adulthood we change, and the brain adapts accordingly, yet we barely notice. "

nothing like the second picture. Yet the individual will continue to be convinced they are looking at the original picture. This person's trust in what they see is steadfast, yet it doesn't align with reality. Metaphorically, this scenario shows a considerable perturbation of the human mind. From birth through childhood and into adulthood we change, and the brain adapts accordingly, yet we barely notice. Our tendencies, preferences, habits, and relationships with people and things change, yet there is a sense of self that never changes. A "witness" self that has been aware of the show the whole time. The question continues to be, who is actually running the show? In the next few sections there are several "hidden" actors in this play whose roles are making a profound impact on everything you do.

Chasing Prisoner #14. Genes

Before delving into epigenetics, we need to understand the role of genes in the body. A thorough reading of the book *Dirty Genes* by Dr. Ben Lynch[46] will give a comprehensive overview of this topic as well as phenomenal action steps to mitigate the problems associated with seven common genetic polymorphisms.

Today, companies like 23 and Me can identify gene single nucleotide polymorphisms (SNPs). After getting your 23 and Me results, go to www.promethease.com to interpret your data. As with the APOE gene alluded to earlier and its relevance to Alzheimer's disease, some of these polymorphisms are incredibly relevant to overall health. The information derived from such tests tend to scare the misinformed. In this case, their thinking is "ignorance is bliss," but the problem is twofold. First, many simply do not understand how probability maps onto genetic polymorphisms. For example, if you receive news that you are 2.3 times more likely to get Alzheimer's disease, it is important to know that the average person has a 1 in 10 chance of getting Alzheimer's.[47] However, only 3.6 percent of that 10 percent get Alzheimer's under sixty-five years old. Therefore, the odds of you getting Alzheimer's before age sixty-five would be .36% x 2.3 = .83% (a less than 1 percent chance). Second, with things like crispr technology[48] on the rise and many other medical advancements, the likelihood of having to worry about many inheritable diseases twenty years from now is minimal. Third, few realize how a simple $199 self-administered saliva test can change your life now. But it can, and it does by simply applying the information derived to your lifestyle. For example, the following common polymorphisms MTHFR, CYP2R1, FUT2, and FADS2 can indicate the following traits:

- MTHFR: Difficulty metabolizing folates
- CYP2R1: Lack of efficiency converting Vitamin D into its active form
- FUT2: Inefficient Vitamin B12 absorption
- FADS2: Inefficiency in the omega-3 fatty acid ALA's conversion to EPA

Consider the common feelings of fatigue and depression. Looking at the four polymorphisms above, contemplate the following: Vitamin D3 acts as a hormone and is involved in about 1,000 metabolic processes. One of D_3's main roles involves serotonin regulation in the gut and in the brain. Serotonin is your "feel good" hormone. Meanwhile, the fatty acid EPA helps release serotonin from neuronal synapses in the brain.[48] Finally, proper methylation of folates along with adequate levels of Vitamin B12 do many critical functions in the body, one of which is assisting overall energy production.[49]

Nevertheless, knowing the specifics of the metabolic pathways is not necessary with 23 and Me. From the results, and with help from a good doctor, you will learn the ill effects of all four polymorphisms might be mitigated through proper sleep and nutrition as well supplementation with the following (listed in order):

- 5L-methyltetrahydrate
- Vitamin D_3
- B_{12} methylcobalamin
- EPA from fish oil

Just five years ago a person could be tired and depressed most days and not understand why. However, with their diet reasonable and exercise vigilant, just the first two polymorphisms would be grounds for fatigue and depression—literally through no free will of their own. Ironically, we now have the ability to identify these mechanisms and address them specifically, yet even when I present this evidence to a room full of people, only about 10 percent will bother testing. It's not because they don't understand or don't have the financial means. It's because they don't opt for a scientifically proven way to feel

> 66
> However, with their diet reasonable and exercise vigilant, just the first two polymorphisms would be grounds for fatigue and depression — literally through no free will of their own.
> 99

better *now*. Sadly, most will choose an on-line shopping binge and half a bottle of wine later that night. Is this free will or an indication of the habits of a *"prisoner chasing 22"*?

Can the personality traits of these prisoners posing as conscious agents be explained genetically? Actually, yes. Looking at just two genes will give incredible insight to personality, emotional tendencies, and likely behavioral patterns. Depending if fast or slow, MAO-A affects mood swings because it governs dopamine, norepinephrine, and serotonin. These critical brain chemicals affect alertness, energy, self-confidence, and even vulnerability to addictions! COM-T, if slow, tends to predict a laid-back and perhaps a little ADHD personality. If fast, this personality is super-focused, but with the strong possibility of "snapping" on the next person who cuts them off in traffic.

What does this information do for you on a practical scale? First, although it may not offer an exculpatory excuse for road rage, it certainly helps you understand your behavior. Instead of wondering, "What the heck is wrong with me?", it's best to realize you're dealing with a different version of a hardware problem (as discussed previously)—but this particular hardware is not your brain, it's your genes. This should not prevent us from making every effort to be the person we want to be in the world, but when undesirable emotions arise, it's far easier to forgive yourself. Furthermore, someone with fast COM-T would be wise to cultivate meditation practices and perhaps listen to calming music while driving. A person with slower COM-T could benefit from something as simple as taking the amino acid L-tyrosine; this remedy is discussed in Dr. Ben Lynch's book, *Dirty Genes*.[50] A simple conversation with a knowledgeable doctor regarding these pragmatic approaches is well worth the potential improvements in quality of life.

Chasing Prisoner #15.
Epigenetics

There's little doubt that a test like 23 and Me is a fantastic way to hack into the biology of your body. However, this is only a part of a much larger story. The larger looming narrative is epigenetics. The easiest way to transition the topic from polymorphic genes to epigenetic expression is by understanding MTHFR's function more specifically. I described MTHFR as part of the methylation process. I said it had several functions, one of which is energy production; however, how this is done is critical to understanding epigenetic expression. Methylation's main role is to suppress gene expression. Genes can be opened or closed or turned on or off like switches. Most of the time we want these switches *off* and the genes *closed*, but sometimes we need them on. Without methylation, 200+ metabolic functions become hampered, including these epigenetic processes. To be clear, MTHFR is not an uncommon polymorphism, and some express it more severely than others. How bad are the expressions of this polymorphism? PubMed research shows studies linking bipolar disorder, severe depression, anxiety, lethargy, and many more to MTHFR.[51]

> " Therefore, can we now begin to understand that free will is starting to look more like a science of overall well-being, offering opportunities of clear thinking? "

Needless to say, epigenetic processes in the body can only be done efficiently when proper nutrition is available. In the case of MTHFR we are talking specifically about methylfolate derived from leafy greens. However, this MTHFR explanation is just a doorway to discuss the bigger story. To recap, I explained a few common gene polymorphisms and how epigenetic expression of genes are only possible via appropriate and specific nutritional compensations. I'll pause here to ask, when you were a child, did you purchase the food for your home? If you were born with a severe expression of this MTHFR gene and the only things available in the house were boxed and frozen goods instead of leafy greens and various fruits, then is your free will expressing MTHFR undesirably? In other words, if you are going into the world feeling tired and anxious because of this polymorphism, it is mostly due to lack of proper nutrition. Therefore, can we now begin to understand that free will is starting to look more like a science of overall well-being, offering opportunities of clear thinking? This conjecture is particularly important as we explore the role of epigenetics and free will.

Hitting the Tongue—Going, Going, Gone!

Back to your childhood refrigerator and pantry for a moment. The human tongue becomes "educated" as you eat a variety of foods and textures throughout your life.[52] This extraordinary tool helps us experience more enjoyment. As we learn to appreciate salty, sweet, sour, and bitter, the tongue plays like a symphony to our brains via electric signals correlating to taste. However, the tongue can become dull and desensitized fairly quickly. If you've ever been on an extended vacation and indulged in desserts more often than you should, then you know coming back to kale salads and curbing carb cravings can prove more difficult. I alluded to the "use it or lose it" axiom earlier in the book, but this is also true of the tongue's ability to appreciate texture and flavor. If, as a child, you had little say on what was hitting your tongue, then I ask once again: It is your free will to have these associated feelings with the MTHFR polymorphism? Furthermore, knowing all this information, how likely is it for a person to hear this, understand it, and continue to eat pizza, pretzels, and candy? In my direct experience, it is *far more likely* for *nothing* to change in their dietary habits long term! The reasons for this are explained later in the book, but again, does the inability to change in light of such profound information sound like free will—or more like the habits of a prisoner chasing 22?

But all of this discussion is still about inside the body. What about the environment outside the body, such as the music you listen to, the TV shows you watch, the people you hang around, the cleanliness of your home, the habits you put in place, and so on? Does this have anything to do with epigenetic expression? The answer is an emphatic *yes*. In fact, I'll argue it is the largest expresser of epigenetics by a long shot. Although no scientist would argue the role of environment outside the body on epigenetic expression, some will not emphasize its role as much as others. But those scientists who choose to deflate the role of epigenetics outside the body largely choose to focus on mouse studies instead of human anomalies, the implications of which I will attempt to explain in detail.

First, let's examine three relevant mouse studies in order to appreciate why a deflationary stance seems appropriate. These three studies are in Nessa Carey's[53] books, *The Epigenetics Revolution* and *Junk DNA*. You can also watch her Ted Talk on YouTube where all three studies are discussed. Note, I am *not* saying Nessa Carey is taking a deflationary stance to epigenetic expression in the environment; I am simply using her fantastic work to explain epigenetic phenomenon. Each of the following studies will likely cause you pause as they further solidify our understanding of epigenetic expression and even free will.

Mouse Study #1

The first study cites how often and how diligently a mother mouse will lick her babies. This is a natural instinct for mice, but some mothers are much better lickers than others. When you examine how these babies react to stress when they get older, it turns out that the babies who were licked more often and more diligently deal with stress far better than their more neglected counterparts. It seems the immediate environment was causing their reaction to the stress. Since the mice could not control how often they were licked at birth, it seems an inevitable conclusion that these mice are doomed to suffer their nurturing dilemma. If you are asking, "Is this an epigenetic argument or a nurturing argument?" that's a good question to be asking; however, I ask you to suspend the question until the last chapter of this section.

Mouse Study #2

The second study involves female mice. These females were being associated with an unpleasant electrical shock each time the smell of cherry blossom was introduced. As you can imagine, it did not take long for these female mice to fear the smell of cherry blossom, yet this is not astonishing news. What is astonishing is that when these female mice gave birth, their children became immediately stressed upon the smell of cherry blossom without ever having been shocked themselves. This is a very clear epigenetic expression through the mother.

Mouse Study #3

The third study is the most telling. I will elaborate on all three of these studies in the next paragraph, but I will use this particular work as a segue to my last points regarding free will in the next chapter. In this third study, a large male mouse was placed in close quarters with a much smaller mouse. This proximity causes the smaller mouse a tremendous amount of anxiety. When the smaller mouse is eventually allowed to breed, the female has babies that are more anxious than other mouse babies. Although this might be another strong argument for epigenetic expression, it is not the most relevant part of this work. Incredibly, if the male mouse is not allowed to mate with the female and instead the male's sperm is extracted and inseminated into the female, something seemingly inexplicable happens. The babies are not born anxious! How could this be? Again, I ask you to table this question for the next section, but it is certainly the most relevant question from this study.

These three studies speak to the power of nurture, environment, and epigenetics. It is no wonder why some scientists downplay the role of environmental epigenetic factors such as the books you read and various lifestyle choices in light of the implications expressed in these mouse studies. It is also no wonder why proponents against free will can look at this evidence and continue to build their case. Yet there is something critical missing from all three of these studies — namely a human mind, and more specifically, a fully developed frontal cortex. The implications of this will be examined later in the book in the section, *Why Does This Knowledge Matter?*

Chasing Prisoner #16. Microbes

If you are unfamiliar with the latest research on microbiota as it relates to human health, please consider looking into the studies of individuals such as Dr. Erica Sonnenburg and Dr. Justin Sonnenburg in their book, *The Good Gut*, as well as Dr. Emeran Mayer's book, *The Mind-Gut Connection*.[54] The microbial biome in the human body is critically important to understand. The large majority of it exists in the form of a tube approximately 24- to 28-feet long (starting at your mouth and ending at your anus). This tube constitutes about 90 percent of all organisms in your body. You are, in fact, mostly microbial, not cellular. This may seem profound if you are unfamiliar with these facts, but I assure you, the profundity is exponential once you understand how these microbes work in the body. To best understand, let us examine one more rodent study.

In their book *The Good Gut*, the Sonnenburgs describe an experiment where they took fecal matter from a healthy, lean rodent and inserted that fecal matter into the anus of an obese rodent. Keep in mind, the lower intestine is where the greatest density of microbes exists in the body; also note they did not change anything else in the rodent's environment, nor did they manipulate its feeding times. Incredibly, the obese rodent began losing weight. Within a few weeks, the rodent was no longer obese. This work has been duplicated many times with similar results. The implications here are astounding, but needless to say, microbes (particularly in the gut) are communicating in a way that is extraordinary. The research of the Sonnenburgs and Dr. Mayer will yield copious evidence regarding the extraordinary tales microbes are telling inside our bodies all the time. Additionally, topics covered in these microbiota studies will include autoimmune disorders, Type-2 diabetes, all forms of digestive issues, all forms of emotional dysfunction, and much more!

There is another important conclusion made in this field dealing specifically with biodiversity. For example, mounting research (such as that being conducted by the Ubiome team)[55] indicates microbial gut diversity is best accomplished through quality and

> " ... microbial diversity is presenting itself as an integral part of overall human health. In fact, diet is one of the main mitigating factors in avoiding the aforementioned diseases correlated with gut-biome health. "

quantity of fiber in the diet. This microbial diversity is presenting itself as an integral part of overall human health. In fact, diet is one of the main mitigating factors in avoiding the aforementioned diseases correlated with gut-biome health. But other research is showing that exposure to a diversity of microbes in the environment is critical to overall immune support as well. For example, it's probably a good idea to lie with your pets, play outside, and interact with lots of different people while leaving the hand sanitizer off your hands. This may seem like a preposterous idea, but ask yourself, how else would an immune system develop unless it learns to advance based on the demands of the environment? This is particularly true for children. Remember, these microbes evolved with us and were around for over a billion years on this planet before us. This is why a healthy exposure to a diversity of microbes is showing benefit in scientific research today. The key is moderation along with a reasonable cost/benefit analysis.

If you are already a germaphobe and find yourself washing all the time, then identify two things you can do to change this mindset. For example, cut down on hand washing and incessant countertop cleaning. Start small and build over time. People who know me know I'm the opposite of a germaphobe. I often eat with my hands, but rarely wash them. I expose myself to lots of different people in a day, sweat on others during Brazilian jiu-jitsu, and will wait until the end of the day to shower. At night, I get under the sheets that I wash only once a week. But ask these same people the last time they saw me sick with even so much as a cold. Some of this may sound extreme, but I'm not asking for extreme, I'm asking for moderation—especially with your children. It's okay if kids get dirty, play with pets, and crawl on the floor. Human beings were doing this for thousands of years, yet today the average two-year-old has already been through three full rounds of antibiotics. Research indicates it can take microbiota a year or more to recover from a single round of antibiotics, yet we are saturating our kids with it. More disturbing, we are doing it while their immune systems are at the most critical stages of development. If a child is learning to walk and falls from time to time, he or she may get bumps and bruises. Is this a reason to stop them from achieving this milestone? Should we relegate them to a swing or constantly hold them to prevent them from harm? Of course not, nor should we be fearful of our children's illnesses and temperatures. Luckily, doctors are now aware of the over-prescription of antibiotics and have begun to back off their administration. Therefore, if you bring your child to the doctor and he/she *does not* prescribe antibiotics, don't be mad—in fact, that physician is likely a keeper!

Third Mouse Study Revisited

Are microbes really all that significant? Stop for a moment to recall the last mouse study in the previous chapter. Here's the recap. When a large male mouse was put in close quarters with a much smaller mouse, the proximity caused the smaller mouse a tremendous amount of anxiety. When the smaller mouse bred, the female had babies more anxious than other mouse babies. Yet, if the male mouse is not allowed to mate with the female, and instead the male's sperm is extracted and inseminated into the female, the babies are not born with this anxious predisposition!

I was unaware of a documented scientific reason for this until I heard Nessa Carey speak on the 27th NCS Podcast Series. After explaining the mouse study to the audience, Nessa claimed, "He (the small mouse) had not epigenetically transmitted his trauma; but rather she (the female mouse) noticed she was breeding with a substandard mouse and somehow or other restricted the supply of nutrients to the offspring." The crowd was astonished by this, and Nessa even paused to acknowledge the rumblings in the audience. Nessa quickly admitted, "We have no idea how this happens." However, I think I might. Ironically, within sixty seconds Nessa stated, "Scientists do this really dumb thing where we say, 'it's my field, that's important, no, it's my field, no, it's my field.'" Her point is that things work together, and so should scientists. Now, based on the few facts I revealed about microbiota, Nessa Carey might follow her own advice and speak to individuals like Justin Sonnenberg or Emeran Mayer. I am willing to bet my bottom dollar that microbes are the culprit.

If you look into the research yourself, I am confident every reader would reach a similar conclusion. When the rodents were allowed to mate, there was proximity, there was penetration, and there was an exchange of fluids. Unbeknownst to most germaphobes, simply being in proximity to other people will create microbe exchange. Obviously, the longer you are around and the more intimate you become the more significant the exchange. My hypothesis need not be true for anyone to

> " All of this being the case, we need to step back and ask some important questions regarding microbes and how this maps onto free will. "

grasp how significant the role of microbes has been throughout history (including plagues, which I discuss later). But more encouraging research shows how these microbes are interacting in our bodies and how we can better improve their functions. All of this being the case, we need to step back and ask some important questions regarding microbes and how this maps onto free will.

Many parents have the good intention of washing their children coming in from play with soap and antibacterial lotions. As parents, we also have the good intention of giving our kids antibiotics when sick. We have the good intention of feeding them their favorite foods when hungry. Yet science is now showing that via these well-intentioned practices, we are also secretly sabotaging their immune system, as well as their overall gut health. This in turn can lead to obesity, insulin insensitivity, and a variety of emotional imbalances as evidenced in the present scientific literature on this subject. I'm not saying these answers are easy. At this juncture, simply grant that via no free will of their own, our children have become victims of belief systems, but this time, belief systems formed within science. Belief systems stemming from the overuse of technology, including (but not limited to) technology in medication, sanitation, and the technology that creates the overabundance of highly processed foods while perpetuating the alarming rate of sugar consumption and,

> " ... technology is not the problem. How we are implementing it, as well as the disproportionate measure with which we rely upon it, are the real problems. "

therefore, disease. But technology is not the problem. How we are implementing it, as well as the disproportionate measure with which we rely upon it, are the real problems. Again, we are ultimately doing this to ourselves and doing it to our children if we don't stop to ask better questions.

Chasing Prisoner #17.
The Forms of Ignorance

There is an important distinction to be made here, but in making this distinction a dramatic turn in the argument for free will unfolds. Namely, the role of ignorance. The word "ignorance" and the word "ignore" both stem from the Latin *ignorare*, "to not know." But today, we use these terms differently. Below I cite four forms of ignorance.

- First, if someone is genuinely unaware of the facts, then ignorance in this context is accurate. I will call this "true ignorance."
- Second, if someone is aware of a situation, but is misinterpreting the circumstances, I will call this "accidental ignorance."
- Third, if someone is blatantly ignoring the truth, this has a very different connotation. Once a person is made aware of the facts and continues to engage in harming themselves, then this person is choosing to ignore the truth. I will call this state of mind "self-induced ignorance."
- Fourth, if someone is made aware of the harm they are doing to others yet continues to engage in deplorable behavior, this I will call "tyrannical ignorance."

The Snake Metaphor[56]

One night Conrad walks down a dark alley between two well-known restaurants in town. To his shock, he sees the body of a giant coiled snake near the dumpster. With his gaze fixed upon the snake, he struggles to peer through the darkness. Gradually his eyes adjust, and with the help the light offered from the front window of Light Side Café, he manages to see the snake's huge triangular head. Frightened, Conrad runs screaming "Giant snake, giant snake!" Everyone in the street, as well as the guests in both restaurants, panic. Some passersby are brave enough to peek for themselves. Sure enough, the massive snake's intimidating size makes those who look upon it have nightmares; for some, the nightmares continue for years! Immediately, rumors circulate via text and social media along with pictures of the obscure coiled snake in the darkness of the alley.

Within ten minutes, nobody is eating in either restaurant and almost nobody is shopping on that street or any of the adjacent streets. The owner of Light Side Café calls the owner of the neighboring restaurant, Dark Thyme's Seasonal Café. The two owners decide to walk out together to investigate. The first owner takes one step into the alley and sees the massive girth of the snake then its triangular head. He runs, hysterical, in the opposite direction toward the safety of his truck. However, the owner of Light Side Café uses a flashlight. Its powerful, narrow beam shines through the blackness and lands upon the snake's body, revealing its true form: an old, coiled fire hose from the volunteer department in the adjacent building. The beam of light slowly moves along the length of the hose. At the tip, a dirty, brass, triangular nozzle that could be easily mistaken for the snake's head. The well-used hose had served its purpose in town for twenty-five years, putting out many fires during its tenure. Now it was being replaced and put next to the dumpster for disposal.

The owner of Dark Thyme's Seasonal Café peers through his truck's window and sees what has been discovered by the beam of light. He sneaks out the passenger side door and creeps from store to store, stealing all unclaimed money and valuables from the now-vacant businesses. It's an opportunity for the perfect heist. This snake metaphor will be revisited at the end of the book with a fresh perspective.

What Happened to Conrad

Keep in mind, the alley was *not* completely dark. The existence of "something" was known; however, Conrad's mind superimposed "snake" onto the hose and nozzle, this is accidental ignorance. Had it been completely dark, the snake would have never been recognized; this would be true ignorance. The giant snake was real to Conrad; as a result, he reacted accordingly. Everyone who heard Conrad would have had the presupposed idea of "snake" in their mind before peering into the dark alley.

Map this scenario onto society. This is how myths come about, yet myths can sell billions of dollars to the uninformed buyer. Simply take a tiny bit of a truth and create an illusion. Diet pills, ab rollers, Thigh-Masters, fad diets, and the like are all ways to sell people on a ridiculous belief, namely, effortless weight loss and a toned physique. Having spent my entire adult life in the fitness industry (while competing at the highest levels of strength in various competitions), I consistently manage a body fat percentage in the single digits. I can assure you, I know what it takes to be strong and healthy. Furthermore, I know what it takes to help others change. Not a little, but a lot. And guess what? It's incredibly hard work! And if you've been paying attention to this free will argument, you are beginning to understand *how* hard.

Back to the metaphor. Only when the beam of light shined on the snake was its true form revealed. But later that night, a different type of snake from Dark Thyme's Seasonal Café lurked in the streets. He used knowledge to his advantage and cost many businesses a lot of money; several would go out of business within a month because of the disturbance. This type of tyrannical ignorance is not relegated to drug dealers or shoplifters. Today and throughout history, tyrannical ignorance has caused more harm from the top down than most would care to imagine. The Catholic popes of the fourteenth, fifteenth, and sixteenth centuries are a good place to start. Police forces in the 1980s and early 1990s as evidenced in the documentary *The Seven Five* are culpable. And of course, politicians and big business have never stopped their demonstration of corruption.

> Today and throughout history, tyrannical ignorance has caused more harm from the top down than most would care to imagine.

What removed the snake? Take a moment to really think about this question. What removed that snake? It was knowledge. Knowledge from the beam of light; metaphorically, from the light of truth. Knowledge from the light brought the awareness to remove the superimposed snake from the harmless hose and nozzle. This form of knowledge is the highest form of truth because it removes illusions and mistakes to reveal what was always there: reality. What we do with the power of understanding is solely up to each of us to demonstrate as parents, friends, and citizens.

All forms of ignorance permeate history, but due to a lack of scientific knowledge, differentiating between accidental ignorance and true ignorance used to hinge on a manifestation exclusively of a human mind: *belief*. Briefly visiting how beliefs have historically shaped these four forms of ignorance, as well as appreciating how they have projected onto others' misery, will give a deplorable account of free will based on bad ideas. Below, two historical events illustrate these circumstances remarkably—and the topic is apropos.

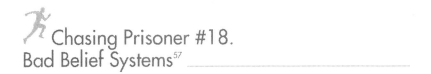

Chasing Prisoner #18.
Bad Belief Systems[57]

From 1338 to 1351 AD, the bubonic plague claimed about one fifth of the planet's population. The body count was so large that Pope Clement VI had to consecrate the Rhone River to use it as a floating cemetery. Nobody knew who or what was causing this epidemic. In alignment with most pre-scientific thinking, the conclusion seemed obvious. The plague must have been a manifestation of God's dissatisfaction with humanity, and punishment would have been a rational conclusion based on circumstances in the world at the time. After all, if God was willing to kill people for merely peeking into the Ark of the Covenant then the savagery of the Mongols was certainly deserving of his wrath. In fact, the plague's origin seems to have stemmed from Mongolia. However, it was not God sending this horrific, painful death to the people he supposedly made in his image. Instead, it was a microbial infection carried by something so small it could barely be seen: a flea.

As trade boomed throughout China and Europe, fleas hitched rides on the bodies of black rats. Before long, people were dying by the millions. All sorts of remedies were tried, including bloodletting and drinking your own urine, while groups of highly religious zealots known as flagellants would beat themselves publicly as a form of penance for sin. But as it turns out, not everyone believed God was punishing the wicked. In fact, Guy de Chauliac chose a very different path toward a possible solution, a path involving rigorous observation, documentation, experimentation, and replication. By the time the plague arrived in Europe, this French pioneer had cultivated an outstanding name for himself as a physician. However, his fame was only made possible due to methods that he based on an emerging way of thinking and understanding the world, what became the foundation of the scientific method.

Unfortunately, despite Guy de Chauliac's relentless studies, the plague continued to ravage the land. It is estimated that one third or more of Europe's population fell victim to this dreadful disease. With no answers in sight and the pope rendered powerless, a desperate Europe searched more vehemently for an answer to the plague's unrelenting death toll. On February 14th in Strasbourg, Alsace, the appalling actions of their citizens culminated in one incredible act of unabated ignorance.

Like fleas, beliefs seem like "little things." We fervently defend our personal beliefs because we think they are our own. But like fleas, many beliefs carry a toxicity unseen by vulnerable minds. The truth is, most people create beliefs based on very bad evidence, and the scapegoat of Strasbourg (as well as much of Europe during this time) illustrates this point precisely and predictably. After hearing the evidence, decide for yourself if this was accidental ignorance or true ignorance.

> Like fleas, beliefs seem like "little things." We fervently defend our personal beliefs because we think they are our own. But like fleas, many beliefs carry a toxicity unseen by vulnerable minds.

Before the plague hit Strasbourg, fearful Christians were hunting and burning Jews who did not convert to Christianity. In doing so, the Christians believed they would earn God's favor. This conundrum is impaneled on two sides by one villain: *belief.* First, the Christian belief that Jews must convert or die. Second, the steadfast belief of the Jews to *not* convert and thus be willing to die. Considering the pedestal on which Jesus has been held for his sacrifice 2,000 years ago, it is ironic to note the uncanny willingness of humans to die to defend a belief in any particular god throughout human history. Whether European crusaders, Scandinavian Vikings, or South American Aztec warriors, all willingly died for some version of their lot in paradise. Nevertheless, on this day, between 1,000 and 2,000 Jews willingly defended *their* faith, but instead of crucifixion and being held on a pedestal throughout human history, they were burned alive. Yet the plague still ravaged the city only a few months later.

This story, and thousands like it, should give us pause. The most dangerous thing on Planet Earth has proven to be the human mind and our largely unchecked belief systems (religious, political, and otherwise). Science has proven time and time again that we can do better with technology. For example, although Guy du Chauliac failed at creating a viable remedy to the plague, he did recognize that keeping a fire burning was wise. He was also able to differentiate between the two forms of plague death, bubonic and pneumonic. And most important, his body of work through his lifetime created the *Chirurgia Magna*, whose seven volumes served as the European standard for medical care for centuries. Today we have much better technology than Guy du Chauliac had 670 years ago; now we can do *much* better. It is time to view thinking as a form of technology—and we all must do better! We should not avoid empowering ideas or beliefs; instead, we must be objective when examining the evidence. We must learn to ask better questions. We must continuously observe and measure the outcomes of our behaviors based on our belief systems. We must start with a desire to mitigate suffering within ourselves and in the world. Is there a more reasonable goal than this?

King of the North?

John Snow is a fictional character in the epic television show, *Game of Thrones*, but history gave us a real John Snow. This John did something extraordinary for his time, and not simply because he helped prevent the spread of cholera. Instead, it was his methodology that earns him high praise.[58] John Snow's brilliance holds the key to help mitigate most human suffering. A profound statement, but I will literally map his brilliance onto a technology of thinking that will be used in the next several sections.

London in 1854 was terribly crowded and saw a horrifying outbreak of cholera, another microbial disease that brings a quick and brutal death. Many watched their young die within hours as bacteria multiplied and ravaged intestines with diarrhea, stomach cramps, and fierce bouts of vomiting. Panic and desperation set in quickly. Many searched for answers, but John Snow had a unique approach. He started mapping where the victims were getting sick and tried to find commonalities. Over a short period of time, he quickly reasoned that the disease was being carried in the water coming out of the Broad Street pump. Despite his best efforts, he could not convince public officials to shut it down. The public relied heavily on the water, and even his best arguments remained suspect.

Nevertheless, John was persistent. A few weeks later, an *anomaly*. He learned of a woman who died of cholera, but she lived in North London. This was too far away from Central London's Broad Street pump to support his hypothesis. It is important to recognize that John could have stopped here and conceded failure. After all, how could someone be sick so far away? There were many water pumps in London, and this unfortunate woman was certainly not getting her water from the Broad Street pump. But John was thorough and *investigated the anomaly*. He went and interviewed the family of the deceased. It turns out that the woman who died was getting her water from her son via the Broad Street pump. Armed with this evidence, the authorities could no longer ignore the likely culprit. Only a few feet from an open sewer, waste would leak through the cracks and crevices in the street until it ultimately went into the water underground. Once the handle from the Broad Street pump was removed, the outbreak stopped.

Why Medicine Still Needs John Snow

Remember Prisoner #5 and the discussion regarding surgical residents working 30-hour shifts? As a reminder: One of the deleterious effects of those following an under-slept lifestyle is that these people are 55% more likely to become obese and suffer the burden of a chronically impaired immune system. Other undesirable outcomes include: poor mental and physical performance, higher likelihood of addiction, increased occurrence of heart attack, and even the development of cancer. It shouldn't take a brain surgeon (no pun intended) to recognize that something needs to change. What would John Snow have done? John would have measured and mapped, then removed the source. But the real conundrum lies within the origins of the policy in the first place. How did such an unorthodox approach become standard practice?

In the late 1800s, the wildly popular surgeon William Halstead, along with his students and fellow physicians, began experimenting on themselves with cocaine (not illegal at the time). It proved to be an effective anesthetic agent. Many, including Halstead, became addicts. Halstead's battle with cocaine and morphine throughout his life is a captivating tale; however, the relevance of his substance abuse on present-day medical policy is what's remarkable.

As a giant in the field, it was well known that Halstead would pay chief attention to the more capable students while blatantly ignoring the rest. As a result, residents would do anything for his approval. His pace in teaching and expectations of them were unrealistically demanding, *including* the hours they worked.

But Halstead was functioning on the most powerful substance to increase alertness known to man. An unfair advantage to say the least, but also a terrible standard for his students to live up to, and an even worse standard upon which to build a policy—but it happened. This extra-long work shift policy has remained a standard of practice in hospitals for five generations—mostly because nobody bothered to question its practicality. Once again, this has proven to be a bad belief system. In the late 1800s, many viewed William Halstead's nonstop work ethic as an anomaly, and like today's Navy Seal training, maniacal methods became the standards upon which surgeons were trained—performance while sleep deprived being one of those standards. However, Halstead wasn't an anomaly in regard to sleep; instead, his body abided by the laws of biology, with a manic work ethic explainable due to cocaine abuse. Ironically, according to those same laws of biology, he became an addict—how apropos.

The medical institutions where the best and brightest minds congregate for the befit of mankind have also fallen victim to the inimical effects of this bad belief system established over 130 years ago. Today we are talking about over 20,000 sleep deprived medical residents in the United States who adversely affect their patient's lives. All of this due to a terrible idea from a brilliant man who also happened to be a cocaine addict. Today, based on all the data, this system simply needs to be uprooted. Apparently, regardless of IQ or degree, nobody is immune from these pervasive mind juggernauts known as bad beliefs. The only possible remedy resides in measuring and mapping while using rigorous science to guide the process.

Chasing Prisoner #19. Anomalies and "Mistakes"

Anomalies happen rarely over the course of a lifetime, but they occur all the time within a population of seven billion on this planet. For example, a star exploding is an anomaly; it happens about once every 100 years in our galaxy. There are about three billion seconds in 100 years. Map that data onto the size of the universe, and dozens of stars are exploding every second. A supernova in this context is no longer an anomaly, it is only an anomaly on a certain scale—

> ... anomalous experiences (of any sort) should be expected from human beings interacting with nature.

even if that scale is the size of the Milky Way. Having said that, anomalous experiences (of any sort) should be expected from human beings interacting with nature — anything from the Aurora Borealis appearing to people in the Caribbean, to beautiful religious experiences, to unexplained genius in music, math, or art. There is nothing unusual about this occurring, in fact, it would be unusual if these things did *not* occur. However, there are *reasons* for these anomalies, and this is where bad thinking can lead to a host of bad beliefs as described during the bubonic plague.

For example, a fourteen-year-old Joseph Smith had an anomalous experience involving buried golden tablets, a seer stone, a magic hat, and the angel Moroni, in the auspicious location of Western New York. This is not a reason to create a religion, nor is there a reason to create a religion around Daniel Tammet's abilities due to his rare form of synesthesia. Asking Daniel if 2,368,469,741 is prime, results in a bizarre sort of quietude before hearing a *yes* or a *no*. Incredibly, he is never wrong! This, despite the fact that the same computers that put men on the moon fifty years ago had no chance of solving that mathematical mystery in any reasonable amount of time. When asked *how* he knows, his answer? "It feels prime."

Whether we are talking about the "feeling" of the prime of numbers, musical symphonies created by children, or a charismatic cult leader like Jim Jones, [59] the truth is, anomalies are happening all the time. The question is, do you understand them?

The Aurora Borealis is happening because charged particles from a solar flare penetrate the earth's magnetic shield and interact with atoms and molecules in the earth's atmosphere. On extremely rare occasions, solar flares are so powerful that these Northern Lights are seen as far south as the Caribbean! Today, we understand synesthesia to be occurring due to excessive interconnectivity in particular areas in the brain. We understand unusual musical ability in much the same way. More specifically, highly religious men like Joseph Smith were likely suffering a temporal lobe seizure, which can induce both hypergraphia and hyper-religiosity. But John Snow was not looking into a magic hat, nor was John drinking anyone's Kool Aid (although if he were a Washing Tongue Adventist, it would likely be cherry flavored), and he was certainly not using the water from the Broad Street pump! John employed mapping and measuring. When an anomaly occurred he thoroughly *investigated*. His tenacity led to the *source* of the problem—in this case, cholera.

Anomalies of Purpose, On Purpose

There are important distinctions to be made between an anomaly occurring randomly due to genetics, brain interconnectivity, the result of head injury such as the case of Jason Padgett, and even Daniel Tammet's abilities that seemed to have arisen due to a series of seizures as a young boy.[60] Nevertheless, none of the anomalies described were "on purpose." More important, many of these "gifts" also come with a "curse." For example, synesthesia is often coupled with difficult or even intimidating social interactions. Simply the way someone speaks certain words, the colors they are wearing, a song playing in the background, or all three of these factors at once, can culminate in an interpretive experience beyond any rational person's wildest dreams.

Is there a way to experience extraordinary anomalies on purpose? Is there a way to experience these anomalies without the "curse"? Absolutely. Speaking for myself, I've recently pushed the limits of extreme cold-water submersion after doing Wim Hof's breathing techniques.[61] But before Wim's ten-week program, I had the advantage of being a meditator since the age of nineteen and I regularly incorporate pranayama yoga into my discipline. I maintain a thorough understanding of breath control, enough to deadlift well over triple my bodyweight in powerlifting competitions. At age forty-two and only 170 pounds, I can hold a 225-pound man standing on my lower back for a full minute while holding a perfectly straight plank position. In my adulthood, I have fasted for two days and recorded myself in meditation for four hours without moving a muscle. Perhaps I cultivated this discipline in high school when I pushed my body to run a 16-minute 5K while earning varsity letters in cross country, basketball, and baseball? Now, despite being a small-business owner for over fifteen years, I muster enough brain power to write books, train clients, and run weekly seminars on health and nutrition, while teaching emotionally disturbed teenagers math and philosophy for nearly twenty years. Oh yeah, and I had a son at twenty-one and a daughter at twenty-four; both of my kids love me to death as I love them. Surely this is an eclectic mix of experiences, disciplines, accomplishments, and rituals, but make no mistake—except for being such a young father, they were *all* on purpose.

But who cares about me? What I've accomplished on purpose is nothing extraordinary. It doesn't stop me from pushing my limits. Looking at the extreme accomplishments of someone like Wim Hof is a starting point for reference of what's possible. But there are so many historical examples! Before 1954, it was believed the human body was physically incapable of running a sub-4-minute mile. Many tried and failed. Science defended these conclusions with evidence in human anatomy and biology. Yet, one man refused to believe this limitation. His name? Roger Bannister.[62] In 1954, Bannister broke the 4-minute mile despite all the evidence ruling against him. Bannister's sheer will power smashed the 4-minute barrier along with the belief systems that defended it. In fact, after Bannister accomplished what was once thought impossible, more than 20,000 runners have achieved this accomplishment—some of them high school athletes!

Bannister and many others in history have proven that obstacles are often a self-imposed limitation. They are examples of "anomalies of purpose on purpose." Here is a personal challenge to *you*. What if you took the practice of meditation as seriously as Bannister took breaking the 4-minute mile? What mental barriers would come falling down? What fears, doubts, anxieties would crumble? What new barriers would arise because of the push toward clarity, truth, and reason? The mind can be pushed. The mind's abilities are far greater than most anyone can conceive. Unfortunately, the common consensus in society is this belief: "That all seems true, but not for me."

My personal challenge to you is this: Read these stories, contemplate, delve deeply into the practices, meditate—then ask yourself if the idea "not for me" or any other limiting belief is true. If you recognize in the core of your being that these *imposed limitations* are not true, then start by asking yourself who or what inside of you has been keeping them alive in the first place?

Start with Measuring Then Mapping and Remapping

John Snow used mapping and measurement as a means to an end. He saw where the problems were, tracked them, counted them, looked for patterns within the map and within people's behaviors; finally, he discovered the culprit. Imagine taking this approach as a means to ameliorate human suffering. At first, this seems like an exercise in psychoanalytical psychology, but with some introspection, we can take the time to understand our beliefs and, therefore, our behaviors. More importantly, we can plan our action and create anomalies of purpose on purpose. The process is often extraordinarily painful in the beginning; however, we can offer ourselves compassion by remembering how many things are influencing our thoughts, actions, and decisions—through no free will of our own.

> The process is often extraordinarily painful in the beginning; however, we can offer ourselves compassion by remembering all the things influencing our thoughts, actions, and decisions—through no free will of our own.

Today, we are at a critical juncture. We have accessibility to an incredible amount of valuable information, but few are willing to filter it, even fewer prepared to implement substantiated knowledge into healthier behaviors. When it comes to free will, are we beginning to understand how societal and parental *accidental ignorance* (today and throughout history) shapes the livelihoods and inevitable lack of free will of our nation and children? If we do not educate ourselves on relevant topics, then we are disallowing the next generation's well-being. We must understand the basics in nutrition, microbes, genetics, epigenetics, and much more. We must understand the causes for concern in certain belief systems, as well as the potential harm in beliefs we hold about ourselves. We *must* do all these things for parents and society to nurture *each other*.

If we don't begin by nurturing each other, life can feel like a monotonous perpetuation of circumstance. In 1348 Europe and 1854 London, death was visiting everywhere, free will was relegated to mere survival. But even today, how much free will does a depressed alcoholic mother of three experience while stuck in an abusive relationship? She barely has money for groceries each week, yet ironically becomes obese due to her incessant sugar consumption. We can all identify with being a victim of circumstance, some more than others. But if we examine this mother's predicament and use mapping and measurement, the lessons learned can be profound.

Chasing Prisoner #20.
Routine

Depression is a serious disorder, and the nature of all addiction is almost always a coping mechanism to deal with extreme stress.[63] A combination of unfortunate circumstances can lead to a lack of self-worth and the acceptance of an abusive relationship. Anyone on the "victim of circumstance spectrum" tends to focus on only *choice* A or *choice* B. Choice A: Sober up, leave the abusive individual, and get a better-paying job. Choice B: Have another drink, keep the job, and accept the abuse from the partner. Choice B offers certainty. It offers routine. Once a predictable routine is established, people can adjust to almost anything.

> Pain ... you get used to pain; the minute you adjust, you can adjust to just about anything, just as long as there's routine, right? Routine ... the human mind in crisis needs it, but if you take it away—that's when you start to lose your shit. (From *The Punisher*, season 1, episode 3, Netflix.)

Again, the brain is wired to survive, not perform. It loves predictability. It does not want to make dramatic and uncomfortable changes. But this type of thinking is precisely the problem entrenched in society, with no methodical remedy other than medication. Long-term medication use is a palliative; it offers no end-game strategy. This is where thinking as a technology is employed—more specifically, mapping and measurement:

> ... the brain is wired to survive, not perform. It loves predictability. It does not want to make dramatic and uncomfortable changes. But this type of thinking is precisely the problem entrenched in society...

The Choice to *See*

As men like John Snow and Guy du Chauliac have demonstrated, there is, in fact, *choice C*. And choice C comes from an ocean of other possibilities. Metaphorically, it is better to call it "Choice *See*." A person in this circumstance would be wise to take a step back to map and measure. To steal a Tony Robbins' quote, "Start by raising just one standard," then see what happens to the rest. For a person with very little money, a trip to the library or borrowing a smartphone for research is a wise choice. If this person hates reading, YouTube is a phenomenal resource with amazing doctors willing to disseminate their expertise for free. Begin by understanding what causes depression, and one will quickly discover that obesity, poor nutrition, a sedentary lifestyle, poor sleep patterns and social stress are some of the main underlying causes. This information is part of the map. Six causes have now been identified, these six are part of the measurement. Let's assume the alcoholic mother of three in the abusive relationship has all six issues. Once research is gathered, practice can begin. When coalesced, the information would look something like this: [64]

Choice See with Basic Nutrition for Depression
- Vitamin D3 is a very cheap supplement and has profound effects on serotonin regulation as well as immune function.
- The fatty acids EPA and DHA in fish oil play a major role on serotonin release and uptake within the brain.

Choice See with a Basic Intervention for Obesity
- Make a conscious effort to drink more water throughout the day and between meals.
- Make a conscious effort to get at least eight hours of sleep each night.

The combination of dehydration and fatigue often couples with feelings of hunger, but this person really just needs to hydrate and rest.

Choice See with a Basic Intervention for a Sedentary Lifestyle
- Commit to a 10-minute walk outside each day, then building over time.

- While walking, practice nasal diaphragm breathing. This breathing has remarkable effects on brain function while getting much-needed exercise.

Choice See with a Basic Intervention for Poor Sleep
- Make sure there is no TV watching or cell phone use before bed or through the night.
- Stopping middle of the night eating is critical.
- The room should be dark.
- A hot bath just before bed forces your body to begin a cool down cycle.
- For most, the room you're sleeping in should be cool.
- Magnesium glycinate before bed is advised (consider that about 80 percent of women are magnesium deficient!).

Choice See to Mitigate Social Stress

It is amazing what can be accomplished with conversation. It is not what is said, but how it is said. Approach each conversation with kindness, and the other party is more likely to take down their walls. This process may take weeks or months to gain traction, but if it is causing severe stress, it is a worthwhile endeavor.

None of this is difficult. Every step is reasonable and based in science. If this person raised one of these standards, he or she would start experiencing more control, certainty, and an overall better daily routine. Think what that would do for a person over time. Let's not stop here.

Choice See for Alcoholism
- Look into Abram Hoffer's work on niacin which is vitamin B3. (There is a flush-free form, but do not buy this form.) It is a very cheap supplement with remarkable outcomes for alcoholics; however, be aware that the flush that niacin causes can be uncomfortable to people at first. Redness and itchiness may accompany intakes over 100 mg; however, in a week to ten days people get used to it and eventually most feel almost nothing at all.
- Since liver stress is a huge concern with alcoholism, consider a cheap supplement like N-acetyl cysteine (NAC); if the financial resources are available, take liposomal glutathione.

- Reducing alcohol should be the goal at first. If this individual is committed to combat depression, then they should understand that alcohol is a depressant. Therefore, dramatically reducing consumption via exact measurement is critical.

Choice See for Groceries

In addressing the grocery dilemma, we can solve several problems at once; however, the grocery problem tends to be a massive addiction within itself, especially in circumstances like this. A quick rummage through the pantry and fridge will likely find sugary, boxed, and bagged foods high in high fructose corn syrup. Sugar is the poison crippling this nation with disease because sugar is an addiction. It works on the dopamine pathways in the brain. However, a committed parent can successfully change her or himself and their children by opting for various root vegetables, leafy greens, and colorful fruits as well as healthy fats such as nuts and seeds. Cheap and smart carb choices are available such as various types of potatoes, beans, and whole grains. Meat once a week is all that is necessary, but I highly encourage purchasing organic meat. Eggs are another great choice of protein, but again, I highly encourage organic. Needless to say, cleaning up the diet in this way is not extraordinarily expensive. The more nutrient-dense the food, the less you need.

Choice See on Getting a Better-Paying Job

The key is finding what you are passionate about and doing it for a living. This will lead to more money and more importantly, more happiness. You must actually show up to the employer to drop your résumé. You must show your enthusiasm. This is why all the other things sabotaging a life must be taken care of as well. You can't convince the employer of your worth if you can't convince yourself. However, if improvements have been made in these other channels then it is much easier to start feeling much better about yourself.

Choice See on Getting Out of an Abusive Relationship

Usually abusive relationships serve as a sort of verbal punching bag: *I go, you go, I go, you go,* and so on. It's a great way to let off steam, but it's an extremely dysfunctional way to behave. Of course, this can escalate to physical abuse. Sometimes people can feel locked into these relationships because of financial needs. This is the worst-case scenario; however, let's look at choice See for the worst case—or any case, for that matter. Take it back to conversation. Think of how different a conversation would be with this partner if the conversation started like this, "I don't want to be this person anymore and I know I need your help to be successful. Can we please help each other accomplish better things?"

But *not* tomorrow, *now*!

Our Addiction to the Worst Thing

But what is it that makes a person hear all this, agree to it intellectually, and then do nothing? For the last time, is this an act of free will, or a prisoner chasing 22? The truth is, people are addicted to being themselves. All the reasons why this is true have been methodically laid out, and I still have not completed the argument. But what is it about right *now*? What is being *accidentally ignored* and constantly eluding us?

> But what is it that makes a person hear all this, agree to it intellectually, and then do nothing? For the last time, is this an act of free will, or a prisoner chasing 22? The truth is, people are addicted to being themselves.

PART III

After having been disturbed, he will be astonished …

Chasing Prisoner #21.
You're Not Who You Think You Are
(The Process of Negation)

Consider the sense of "me-ness." This sense of "I." At this point, the topic of free will has revealed a lot of flaws with our sense of agency in the world. Circumstances and nurturing aside, consider simply the biology of free will. Now, consider this sense of self. Who is deciding? Who are you? Are you deciding, or are your genes deciding? Are you deciding, or is your past deciding? Are you deciding, or are your habits, addictions, and hormones deciding? Are you feeling this way, or is it mental illness or maybe just the music? But here's a better question: Who is thinking your thoughts? Who is choosing the thoughts for you to think?

> " But here's a better question: Who is thinking your thoughts? Who is choosing the thoughts for you to think? "

Earlier, I left the John Nash story on a cliffhanger. If you don't recall, John claimed to have cured his schizophrenia by "willing it away." Understandably, many would claim this to be a true act of free will; however, who thought that thought for John? Where did that thought come from? Did he choose that thought? Certainly, he thought this thought many times over the decades and deemed it useless—so why now? Is this free will, or is it something else?

When it comes to thought, we should ask, who or what is aware of thought? Consciousness is undoubtedly our best case of who we *really* are; however, let's be strict about defining consciousness.[60] Every time I hear a philosopher or scientist talk about consciousness, I hear them describing more "brain stuff." I acknowledge that consciousness may be an emergent property of the brain (this topic is known as the hard problem of consciousness), but even if consciousness is an emergent property, it's unhelpful to speak about it *pragmatically* as anything other than awareness. If we keep reducing consciousness and ultimately find the "holy grail" causation, it's still unhelpful to think of consciousness as anything other than awareness. As far as a human is concerned, consciousness is the

> As far as a human is concerned, consciousness is the underlying substratum upon which everything exists ... But to call this conscious witness the "Self" is also a mistake. As we will see, the Self, too, is merely an illusion.

underlying substratum upon which everything exists, meaning that all our experiences depend upon this underlying conscious witness. But then to call this conscious witness the "Self" is also a mistake, because, as we will see, the Self, too, is merely an illusion. Metaphorically, consciousness is the electricity allowing the software (your brain) to run on the computer hardware (your body).

You've Been Living in a Dream World, Neo

Today, some theoretical physicists are focusing on this exact assumption: You may be living in a computer simulation. If this possibility seems absurd, please look into the works of philosophers like Clement Vidal and Nick Bostrom. For a layman's perspective, watch Neil deGrasse Tyson's interview with world-renowned theoretical physicist Brian Greene on *Star Talk* (season 4, episode 6). Finally, check out episode 6, season 4 of Morgan Freeman's *Through the Wormhole*. After watching, let me know if you'd like to swallow the red or blue pill. If you're not understanding these references to the original *Matrix* (1999), then add that to your must-watch list as well!

Glitches in the Matrix?
A Brief Science and Miracle Metaphor

Entertain the computer simulation construct for one more paragraph in order to consider a better stance on science and miracles. If in a simulation, we wouldn't know what a glitch would look like, and even if we did, a programmer could easily fix the error without anyone in the program knowing. But revisiting Jason Padgett's and Derek Amoto's stories could prove interesting. Any glitch would have to occur in the mind of the individual experiencing the glitch. In the case of Jason or Derek, it may seem they are experiencing a glitch in the system; furthermore, anyone observing their unexplainable talents could see this as a glitch and objectively confirm its validity. Yet we can explain both anomalies (and others like them) via science. A true glitch would be if a person was struck in the head and could suddenly fly or walk through walls, because it would be impossible for science to explain how this happened. It would constitute a "miracle," but much to the chagrin of the highly religious, no miracle has even been proven to occur, despite the million-dollar Randi paranormal bounty[66] awarded to anyone who can perform said miracle without scientific explanation. It's hard enough to stump Penn and Teller but even harder to stump science.

Or Were You Looking at the Woman in the Red Dress?

Of course, many con artists in the past have tried to claim paranormal powers and prize money. One story involving Harry Houdini and the famous Boston medium, Mina Crandon, gives insight into an aspect of human experience that truly underscores reality.[67] Ms. Crandon made quite a name for herself through the paranormal. For years, she led séances in Boston and was nearly the recipient of a cash prize offered by the *Scientific American* committee. It didn't take Houdini long to suspect what was happening in the act. But the question is, *how* did Harry figure it out? Similarly, how do Penn and Teller figure out the acts on their TV show *Fool Us?* First, it's important to understand that no doctor, physicist, or psychologist on the *Scientific American* board could figure out what Houdini discovered. In the same way, nobody other than a highly skilled and experienced magician could do what Penn and Teller do. But that's not as important as understanding *how* most magic tricks actually work. In the case of Mina Crandon, Houdini went into the séance knowing the art of distractibility and its effect on the mind. Essentially, most magic tricks work by diverting attention, but Harry Houdini was never distracted by "the woman in the red dress," nor was he distracted by Mina's antics, which eventually helped prove her as a fraud.

The Real Magic Trick

As evidenced throughout this book, the entire world behaves like a magic trick. The differences between us ultimately come down to how well we pay attention and what we are paying attention to most of the time. Going back to Tristan Harris (former design ethicist at Google), read what he says in this analogy referencing how companies drive time on site.

> "As evidenced throughout this book, the entire world behaves like a magic trick. The differences between us ultimately come down to how well we pay attention and what we are paying attention to most of the time."

> What people miss about this is, it's not by accident; the web and all of these tools will continue to evolve to be more engaging and to take more time because that is the business model. And so, you end up in this arms race for essentially who's a better magician, who's a better persuader, who knows these back doors in people's minds as a better way of getting people to spend more time (on site).
> —Tristan Harris (Sam Harris Podcast #71)

If we are constantly distracted by the next thing to fill our fleeting desires, then it's easy for us to lose sight of what actually matters. As soon as that happens, you're a victim of the show instead of an objective master who understands the illusion (like Houdini). Keep in mind, everyone watching a magic show knows it's magic, but this does not prevent the audience from being entertained. If you delve into the inner

> Delving into the inner workings of magic does not ruin the show; instead, like Penn and Teller, you can appreciate how well magicians perform … In the same way, you can be more objective to free will — and to life for that matter.

workings of magic it does not ruin the show; instead, like Penn and Teller, you can learn to appreciate how well the magician performs the trick. You can step out of the magic show and discover how to do magic. In the same way, you can be more objective in regard to free will—and to life for that matter. This will allow you to discover something special about your relationship to life, and to the world around you. Whether you are in the audience or on the stage, whether you are in the Milky Way galaxy or plugged into the matrix, don't be a fraud—instead, make the conscious choice to play your part well!

Negation 101

If "The Matrix" possibility seems ridiculous as grounds for negation, no problem. Instead, take an introspective approach. A brief mind experiment is beneficial. So, please just get comfortable and contemplate each of the following:

- You have a human body.
- It is a body made from food and fluids that you consume.
- You are experiencing the world through five senses.
- These five senses are being interpreted by a human brain.
- The brain is using electric and chemical signals to interpret reality.
- Underlying these mechanisms is the experience of what seems to be "uniquely you," but this particular sense of "you" is actually just a lot of body and brain phenomenon.

• This "you" is an illusion based on how various forms of matter are interacting within the body and brain.

There remains one thing to further investigate (at least for now): consciousness. But for now, consider consciousness as "witness self" with *nothing* added to it. As soon as we add something to consciousness we are, by definition, talking about experience. Therefore, all experiences can be negated. Why? Because from this context (as well as your own direct empirical knowledge), every experience is inherently something other than you. It is an experience happening in consciousness.

If consciousness turns out to be an emerging property of the brain, all of the underlying points about consciousness remain. Similarly, if we are in a computer simulation, all points remain. More importantly, in either case, we can more accurately state: Every *"thing"* is just experience appearing in consciousness, including your experience of "self." Therefore, even your experience of "self" is ultimately an illusion that is appearing in and dependent upon consciousness.

Take your time digesting that last statement; it's a doozy. But remember the promise: *"When he does find, he will be disturbed."* Regardless of any perspective on consciousness, all we have and all we will ever have is experience, and these experiences are happening in our minds. Therefore, the mind is the most important tool to keep healthy, to sharpen and master. Having read all the arguments ascribed in the free will section, you don't need more reasons to occasionally distrust your brain. Negation proves to be a critical component in discovering a deeper aspect of being, namely the "witness self," and ultimately, the witness self as part of the grand illusion. There is, in fact, *only* experience.

> " Regardless of any perspective on consciousness, all we will ever have is experience, and these experiences are happening in our minds. Therefore, the mind is the most important tool to keep healthy, sharpen and master. "

PART IV

Then he will reign over everything …

Why Does This Knowledge Matter?

If we are going to utilize technologies in thinking such as *mapping and measuring, anomalies of purpose on purpose, experiencing a choice* See, as well as any notion of free will, then the starting point should not be in the storm (as discussed in the captain of the "Bull-Ship" metaphor). Nor should you concede to "being the storm," as Sam Harris suggests in his book, *Free Will* (2012). By now, what we should concede is that free will is in turbulent, muddy waters. Through all this interference, we are straining to find some reflection of "I." But the more we peer into the dark, murky disturbance, the more this sense of "me" begins to present as an illusion. Instead, we must find a better starting point—not in the storm, or of the storm, but in the silence. Within the silence a process can begin. In that silence, give the mind direction for the purpose of contemplation.

> " But the more we peer into the dark, murky disturbance, the more this sense of "me" begins to present as an illusion. Instead, we must find a better starting point—not in the storm, or of the storm, but in the silence. "

As a starting point, evaluate the following three things about consciousness, awareness, or "I-ness":

- Consciousness is always in the present moment. It is always "now"; therefore, the present moment is eternal.
- Anything to be known can only be known "now." If the mind is constantly in a daydream, then nothing new is gained. The present moment offers a much deeper reality for a human being without all the extraneous superimposed delusions of the mind.
- It is impossible to have a problem "now." All problems are projections of the past or the future. Any solution to a problem can only be solved in the now. Therefore, all knowledge exists in the now.

Next, review the following three things about silence and stillness:

- We only hear sound because there is a silence that sustains it.
- We only recognize movement because there is stillness for comparison.
- We experience "noise" in the mind in the form of thoughts, yet underneath is a still and silent "witness" that is aware.

If God has the attributes of knowledge, truth, and is everlasting, then the present moment seems a good place to seek whatever we are calling "God." Perhaps this sort of intelligence *and* present-moment conscious observation should be explored more thoroughly? For example, *the five senses only operate in the present moment.* Choosing to work through the senses by becoming acutely aware of whatever is in front of you is an easy way to gain presence of mind now. If listening to another person speak, then fully listen to the sound of their voice. If you are speaking, then fully listen to the sound of your own voice. If you are washing dishes, be present with the sense of touch with each spoon, dish, and glass. This is a skill to cultivate, but within that intense state of presence an entire world will unfold, free of anxiety, depression, and fear. It is reality with much less background noise. When attention is on the task at hand via the conscious use of the senses, the result is more clarity, more efficiency, and less opportunity for the mind to rehearse its whimsical and often self-critical/self-destructive behavior.

It's Okay to Not Know

In the beginning of the book, I stated we need to understand what free will is *not*. I think that mission has been accomplished. The truth is, we don't know if free will exists. But it's okay to not know! Would you rather have questions you don't know the answer to, or answers you don't know how to question? If your answer is the latter, there may be a seat for you at the Washing Tongue Adventist lodge. Sarcasm aside, the truth is that I take human existence seriously, but more accurately, I take my responsibility to help mitigate human suffering much more seriously. I recognize my blessings, and if people are going to change the world, it's largely going to be the most educated people in the most fortunate circumstances. Therefore, if we are going to make a case for freedom, let us always keep in mind these arguments put forth regarding this notion of free will, because it must begin with full presence of mind. It must be happening *now*. As obvious at that may seem, simply practice watching your mind and ask yourself, "How often am I consciously invoking my will into the world?" I encourage you, at every moment, act as if you have free will!

> As obvious at that may seem, simply practice watching your mind and ask yourself, "How often am I consciously invoking my will into the world?" I encourage you, at every moment, act as if you have free will!

What the Experts Missed in Free Will

I spent the entire book playing devil's advocate with free will. Recognizing the tidal wave of influences against our sense of agency in the world is critically important to understanding human behavior. But I feel strongly that there is something in this haystack we are missing. I'm talking about practice. More specifically, I'm referring to the fact that all our lives we have been

> Due to lack of outside influences to help us think greater thoughts or question underlying beliefs about ourselves, we have allowed the world to present free will like a Santa Claus.

rehearsing the same role. We have been practicing being who we believe ourselves to be. Due to lack of outside influences to help us think greater thoughts or question underlying beliefs about ourselves, we have allowed the world to present free will like a Santa Claus. As evidenced in this book, we have accepted belief systems about justice, health, economic status, mental illness, and so much more in the same manner a Washing Tongue Adventist accepts his beliefs about George Washington. In other words, when we really examine decisions, thoughts, behaviors, movement, and so on, it is clear we don't know exactly where they are coming from or how they are happening. However, consider that *anything* you practice over and over again yields that same result. For example, with enough *practice*, playing the piano beautifully begins to feel like you are not the do-er—in fact, that is the goal!

Yes, We Are Talking about Practice

I know it's important, I do, I honestly do, but we talkin' about practice man. What are we talkin' about? Practice? We talkin' about practice, man. We talkin' about practice, we talkin' about practice—we ain't talkin' about the game—we talkin' about practice, man.

—Allen Iverson (May 7th, 2002 press
conference, after missing practice)

When you move, when you decide, when you think, it is all occurring from what's been practiced. But what if we can practice training our minds in the same way? In order to do this, reexamine the first words of the book: We need "information, information, information," but not just any information, we need better information in order to *better* understand reality.

What We Missed in the Snake Metaphor

Recall the snake metaphor. The beam of the flashlight removed the superimposed "snake" from the mind. Metaphorically, the light of truth was projected onto the snake and allowed the mind to see the snake's true form, a mere hose. Today, consciousness experts eloquently demonstrate that reality is not simply interpreted from the outside in (as evidenced in the snake metaphor), but also from the inside out. Throughout this book, you've learned how manipulations of reality can be extremely subtle, sometimes accidental and often through no free will of your own. But reconsider the snake metaphor. Yes, the snake's true form can be revealed via the beam of light; yet, there are other ways to identify the snake's true form without an "outside in" approach. For example, Conrad was a safe distance from the snake. If he paused to consider his situation, perhaps a few facts would have resonated. First, Conrad had a jacket on, it was winter. Snakes do not come out in the cold. Second, he lives in Connecticut. Snakes the size of a fire hose don't live in Connecticut; in fact, a snake that size does not exist anywhere in North America. Finally, the sign for the fire house was just above the dumpster. Through contemplation, Conrad could have realized that the coiled object was not a snake. Upon more careful inspection of his environment he could have reasoned that he was staring at an old hose from the firehouse. This is one way for an inside-out interpretation to more predictably align with reality. Another way is through conversation; however, the company you keep would need to offer these same levels of insight. For example, if Conrad had been frightened by the snake while walking with his girlfriend, Peyton, perhaps *she* would have been the one to say, "There's no way that's a snake, Conrad, it's the middle of winter." On the other hand, if Conrad were walking with Joseph Smith, that fire hose was likely to be the snake from the Garden of Eden and even more likely to have whispered a few sweet nothings in his ear.

To reiterate, we don't merely need

> To reiterate, we don't merely need more information. The world is full of information. Today, we need better information, we need contemplation, we need good company, but we also need better practice.

more information. The world is full of information. Today, we need better information, we need contemplation, we need good company, but we also need *better* practice. Wait, are we talking about practice again? Yes, I'm talking about practice. To appreciate the practice to which I'm referring, consider this metaphor:

The Practice

Start by just sitting. (Yes, just sit). Now, close your eyes for one minute and just breathe. Go ahead, do it! Now, simply acknowledge you have been breathing your whole life without having to think about it. This time, close your eyes and take ten deep breaths through your nose. But after each deep breath hold it for a while and then exhale that air out of your nose with control. Allow all stress and negativity to leave the body with each exhalation. Go ahead. *Practice*. Do it *now*.

Notice you imposed your will into the breath in each moment? You did it with a specific instruction and intention. If free will exists, it must exist in the same way that breath exists. In other words, if you aren't practicing "doing life," then life is being done "to you." Similarly, if you aren't breathing then breathing will be done for you. Therefore, it is best to pick and choose some time during each day to practice "doing life." Choose it consciously and choose it often, but to do it at all, it's best to have a method

> " If free will exists, it must exist in the same way that breath exists. In other words, if you aren't practicing "doing life," then life is being done "to you." Similarly, if you aren't breathing then breathing will be done for you. "

such as creating your environment, invoking proper nutrients and supplementation for the health of the brain and body, as well as using the five senses as described earlier. Because, ladies and gentlemen, *if free will exists, it is a matter of proper practice and biology gone right.*

For John Nash, it took decades for his biology to get "right enough" to ignore the voices in his head. But we all have those voices; they exist on a spectrum of disturbance. For a schizophrenic, these voices inhibit normal functioning in the world, but the voices in everyone's heads inhibit willful functioning in the world—and this is through no free will of your own. The only way to turn down the volume is to invoke knowledge. Use choice See to improve your environment, nutrition, and belief systems. Use mapping and measuring to create new habits and skills. This will improve the biology of the body and mind to work for you, instead of against you. An autoimmune disorder is when the body attacks itself; as a result, the body gets sick.[68] Similarly, how can a mind invoke free will if its biology is consistently at war with itself? Create the space, sit with the silence, observe your mind, and understand you are not your thoughts. Then breathe—as if for the first time, breathe conscious breaths and leave the world behind. Allow yourself the freedom to experience yourself in a fresh way then build on it objectively without attachment to the result. Consciously choose to challenge yourself, push yourself, be determined to master the biology of your body and brain. Most importantly, enjoy the ride, wherever it leads!

> " Consciously choose to challenge yourself, push yourself, be determined to master the biology of your body and brain. Most importantly, enjoy the ride, wherever it leads! "

Throughout this book, I hope the knowledge and its benefits were self-evident. Examining topics as thoroughly as possible is necessary. If, for example, you have lived your entire life never thinking about free will then I would argue we must do better! After all, if there is one thing that makes us uniquely human, it is this aspect of existence! The information in this book will grow on you, but to be clear, this information will not necessarily become self-evident to merely-curious readers. Instead, the real benefits will go to the courageous practitioners willing to do the work. If anything is going to change, it needs to start with some reasonable, well-designed action.

Chasing Prisoner #22.
Understanding

Finally, if you still take umbrage to some or all these arguments regarding free will, then take a moment to ruminate on one more aspect of free will. Simply recognize that every word you just heard or read was understood by no free will of your own. Like the complexity of movement discussed earlier, your mind simply understood—and furthermore, it understood a complex topic with no conscious "doing" on your part. All of this is quite remarkable, in fact, it's miraculous. But if you're making an exceptional effort to ignore what's being offered because it trespasses on a belief system, then I forgive you, because it is precisely this type of thinking which is of no free will of your own.

FOOTNOTES

1. Sam Harris podcast, Waking Up with Dr. Robert Sapolsky, Episode 91, "The Biology of Good and Evil."

2. Though the Wormhole, Season 3, Episode 8, "Mysteries of the Subconscious."

3. America: The Story of Us, Season 1, Episode 2, "Revolution."

4. David Eagelman, The Brain (New York, Pantheon Books, 2015).

5. https://www.test-iq.org/iq-scores-and-iq-levels/

6. http://news.gallup.com/poll/166211/worldwide-median-household-income-000.aspx

7. https://www.unicef.org/publications/files/UNICEF_SOWC_2016.pdf

8. Ibid, UNICEF.

9. Eagelman, The Brain, 8.

10. Judith Rich Harris, The Nurture Assumption (New York, Free Press, 2009). Chapter 7.

11. Mina Cikara in Through the Wormhole, Season 6, Episode 1, "Are We All Bigots?"

12. Stephen G. Bloom, "Lesson of a Lifetime," Smithsonian Magazine, September 2005, https://www.smithsonianmag.com/science-nature/lesson-of-a-lifetime-72754306/

13. Ibid., Through the Wormhole, "Are We All Bigots?"

14. Eagelman, The Brain, p. 16.

15. Nessa Carey, The Epigenetic Revolution (New York, Columbia University Press, 2017). Chapters 1 and 6.

16. Dr. Robert Sapolsky, Why Zebras Don't Get Ulcers (3rd ed.) (New York, Henry Holt, 2004). Chapter 6, "Dwarfism and the Importance of Mothers."

17. Dr. Daniel Amen has many books on the brain and brain injury. His website, http://www.amenclinics.com/ has specific information regarding concussions and traumatic brain injury. He also has a TEDx Talk addressing these topics: "The Most Important Lesson from 83,000 Brain Scans," https://www.youtube.com/watch?v=esPRsT-lmw8

18. Joe Rogan Podcast, The Joe Rogan Experience, Episode 568, with Dr. Rhonda Patrick.

19. Jason Padgett & Derek Amato, The Consciousness Chronicles, 3 DVD "Synesthesia."

20. The role of luck in free will is highlighted by many authors; this is nothing novel.

21. Through the Wormhole, Season 5, Episode 2, "Is Luck Real?"

22. Shai Danziger, Jonathan Levav, and Liora Avnaim-Pesso, "Extraneous Factors in Judicial Decisions." Proceedings of the National Academy of Sciences, 2011. http://dx.doi.org/10.1073/pnas.1018033108

23. Sam Harris Podcast, Waking Up with Dr. Robert Sapolsky, Episode #91, "The Biology of Good and Evil."

24. Corpus callosum studies: http://www.jhrr.org/text.asp?2014/1/2/27/150793 These experiments are also discussed in: Sam Harris Podcast, Waking Up with Robin Hanson, Episode #119, "Hidden Motives."

25. Matthew Walker, PhD, Why We Sleep: Unlocking the Power of Sleep and Dreams (New York, Scribner, 2017).

26. Ibid., Walker.

27. Dr. Rhonda Patrick Podcast, Found My Fitness, Episode with Don Pardi, "Sleep, Daylight Anchoring, and Effects on Memory and Obesity."

28. Joe Rogan Podcast, The Joe Rogan Experien ce, Episode 1108, with Matthew Walker.

29. Ibid., Rogan.

30. The American Experience, "A Brilliant Madness." Documentary on the life of John Forbes Nash Jr. PBS, 2012.

31. John Nash's quote about conformity would have been, "And truly it demands something godlike in him who has cast off the common motives of humanity and has ventured to trust himself for a taskmaster. High be his heart, faithful his will, clear his sight, that he may in good earnest be doctrine, society, law, to himself, that a simple purpose may be to him as stone as iron necessity is to others!" (Ralph Waldo Emerson, Self-Reliance)

32. Sam Harris Podcast, Waking Up with Dr. Robert Sapolsky, Episode #91, "The Biology of Good and Evil."

33. Jim Fallon, Through the Wormhole, Season 3, Episode 7, "Can We Eliminate Evil?"

34. Sam Harris Podcast, Waking Up with Dr. Robert Sapolsky, Episode #91), "The Biology of Good and Evil," and Waking Up with Dr. Daniel Dennett, Episode #39, "Free Will Revisited."

35. Anosognosia, also called, "lack of insight," is a symptom of severe mental illness experienced by some that impairs a person's ability to understand and perceive his or her illness. See http://www.treatmentadvocacycenter.org/key-issues/anosognosia

36. Sam Harris Podcast, Waking Up with Dr. Daniel Dennett, Episode #39, "Free Will Revisited."

37. Dr. Dennis Schafer, Through the Wormhole, Season 4, Episode 9, "Do We Have Free Will?"

38. Sapolsky, Why Zebras Don't Get Ulcers. Chapter 15, "Personality, Temperament, and Their Stress-Related Consequences," and Chapter 18, "Managing Stress."

39. Jonathan Shay, MD, PhD, Achilles in Vietnam: Combat Trauma and the Undoing of Character. (New York, Simon & Schuster, 1995).

40. Sam Harris Podcast, Waking Up with Tristan Harris, Episode #71, "What Is Technology Doing to Us?"

41. Tristan Harris, "How Technology is Hijacking Your Mind"—from a Magician and Google Design Ethicist. Thrive Global, May 18, 2016.

42. V. S. Ramachandran, PhD. Consciousness (DVD), Alsbury Films.

43. The C-major chord followed by a C-augmented chord:
https://www.edmprod.com/different-chord-types/
https://www.youtube.com/watch?v=etNHA3RhDo8

44. Henrik Ehrsson, Through the Wormhole, Season 3, Episode 8, "Mysteries of the Subconscious." Henrik Ehrsson's work is also explained in Consciousness Chronicles 2 (DVD), "The Future of Avatar Development."

45. Sam Harris Podcast, Waking Up with Anil K. Seth, Episode #113, "Consciousness and the Self."

46. Ben Lynch, MD, Dirty Genes. (New York, Harper One, 2018).

47. Odds of Alzheimer's: https://www.mayoclinic.org/diseases-conditions/alzheimers-disease/symptoms-causes/syc-20350447

48. Jennifer A. Doudna and Samuel H. Sternberg, A Crack in Creation. (Boston, Houghton Mifflin Harcourt, 2017).

49. Dr. Rhonda Patrick's website, www.foundmyfitness.com, is filled with interviews of other doctors as well as her own videos. She has done primary research on vitamin D3, and most of her interviews involve this topic.

50. Lynch, Dirty Genes, chapters 6 and 8.

51. C. Y. Hu, Z. Z. Qian, F. F. Gong et al., "Methylenetetrahydrofolate reductase (MTHFR) Polymorphism Susceptibility to Schizophrenia and Bipolar Disorder: An Updated Meta-analysis." Journal of Neural Transmission (Vienna, Austria). February 2015; 122(2):307–320. doi:10.1007/s00702-014-1261-8.

52. S. S. Schiffman, S. D. Pecore, B. J. Booth et al. "Adaptation of Sweeteners in Water and in Tonic Acid Solutions." Physiology & Behavior, 1994; 55(3):547–559

53. Carey, The Epigenetic Revolution.

54. Dr. Erica Sonnenburg and Dr. Justin Sonnenburg, The Good Gut (New York, Penguin Books, 2016), and Dr. Emeran Mayer, The Mind–Gut Connection (Harper Wave, 2016).

55. The U-biome Project: www.ubiome.com

56. I learned of the snake metaphor through study of Adi Shankara's work. Although he lived over 1,200 years ago, his contribution to Eastern thought is unparalleled. Almost all commentaries on major Vedanta scriptures today have been the work of Adi Shankara.

57. Mankind, The Story of All of Us, Season 1, Episode 5. "Plague." The History Channel, and "The Black Death: The World's Most Devastating Plague," The Great Courses, 2016.

58. The History of All of Us, Season 1, Episode 10, "Revolutions."

59. Jonestown: The Life and Death of Peoples Temple (PBS Documentary, 2006).

60. Brainman. The Science Channel (documentary, 2005). Daniel Tammet's whole story should be watched carefully. There are other stories of synesthesia in this documentary, but Daniel's is one of the most extraordinary anomalies I've ever seen. About seventeen minutes in, they give the "scientific" explanation of synesthesia, but I'll leave it up to you to decide if these explanations are adequate. Other stories are also heard in Superhuman: Geniuses. (Extraordinary People. Documentary).

61. Wim Hof: www.wimhofmethod.com

62.. Bannister: Everest on the Track, Virgin, 2016. Available on www.bannisterdocumentary.com

63. Sapolsky, Why Zebras Don't Get Ulcers, Chapter 14, "Stress and Depression."

64. For more information on nutrition and behavioral interventions please see my manuals: Thomas Phillips, The Ultimate Transformation Challenge (2018)

65. A few experts on consciousness include: David Chalmers, Anil K. Seth, Daniel Dennett, Christof Koch, Roger Penrose, and Stuart Hameroff.

66. The Million Dollar Randi Paranormal Challenge was issued by James Randi Educational Founder (JRF). It started in 1964 as a $10,000 prize and grew to $1,000,000 after his friend Rick Adams donated $1,000,000 toward the prize. The prize was left unclaimed after over fifty years.

67. Mina Crandon and Houdini - http://www.prairieghosts.com/margery.html

68. Donna Jackson Nakazawa, The Autoimmune Epidemic (New York, Touchstone, 2008).

Made in the USA
Middletown, DE
03 August 2018